LIFE IS A

Cycle

A true story of resilience, cycling adventures and solo travel.

To John

[signature]

www.sineadekennedy.ie

ISBN: 978-1-7393002-0-3
eBook ISBN: 978-1-7393002-1-0

LIFE IS A
Cycle

A true story of resilience,
cycling adventures and
solo travel.

This book is dedicated to anyone who has ever felt lost in life.

Contents

Acknowledgements

Without thinking how long it would take me to write this book, or how difficult it would be, I started with a pen and paper in Cuba, December 2019. I never imagined it would take me three years to complete the task in hand. Talk about being naïve!

Thankfully, I had plenty of amazing people around me to help me through the entire process. I am eternally grateful.

I would like to thank Mary Whelan for dragging the stories out of me. Claire Dalton, Barbara McGuiness, Anne Marie Mc Donald, Liz Turley and Hilary O'Dea for reading the book numerous times and spotting many inconsistencies.

A huge thanks goes to Tom Weymes who proofread this book more times than I am sure he would ever have liked to. His minutely careful amendments were accepted graciously and while I will never be an academic, I have learnt from Tom the importance of good grammar and punctuation.

Without Peter Naessens expert design this book would still be a Word document! Special thanks to Gavin Duffy, Brian Manners and Ivan O'Brian for their extensive professional input.

Finally, I would like to thank my parents wholeheartedly for always being there for me. I know I wasn't always easy to get along with, but you never gave up on me. You made me who I am, and I know you secretly brag about me and my achievements to anyone who will listen!

"She flies with her own wings."

-*Jesse Quinn Thornton*

Chapter 1
Enough was enough.
Dublin, January 2005

Sometimes life is hard. Other times it's complicated. However, when the shit hits the fan and life becomes a total mess, that's when all hell breaks loose! That's what happened to me. I was juggling too many balls and one day I dropped them all. I was overwhelmed, exhausted, mentally burnt out and was sick of everything going wrong. In the space of one week I bought a house I couldn't afford but the bank gave me the money anyway. That was Monday. On Friday I was dumped by my boyfriend. He explained it was due to a number of reasons, but the main issue was because I was totally unpredictable. He never knew what was going to come out of my mouth next and he couldn't cope with that! On Saturday, because my week wasn't going badly enough, without warning my job ceased to exist. Apparently, after working like a dog all over Christmas they didn't need me in January. It felt like I was disposable and didn't matter to anyone. I was living in a hellish, fickle society that only cared if I was on the property ladder or not. I hated that life. Every single bit of it.

"Sometimes it takes a good fall to know where you stand."

-Hayley William

Chapter 2
Caterpillar to butterfly
Dublin, September 2005

I felt completely lost. I was slumped on a bench in the small, utterly depressing excuse of a garden they provided. The four walls that enclosed it reached so high into the sky that they drowned out any possibility of seeing the sun. The garden was so drab and dire that even weeds couldn't be bothered to grow there. It was soulless, which matched exactly how I was feeling. Like a statue I sat there, numb, staring into space. I was in complete shock and disbelief that I had ended up inside that place "for my safety."

Just a few days before I had given up completely, life was too hard, and I wanted out. It was the only solution I could find to stop the torture that living was causing me. I didn't like myself in the slightest and I just couldn't face feeling that way anymore. I had done my best to soldier on from the crap January had thrown at me, but in all honesty, I was just going through the motions and dying a slow death on the inside.

Without any hesitation or regard for my decision, I had taken matters into my own hands. However, I couldn't even manage to get that right. In my eyes, everything I touched was a failure, including myself. As a result of my actions, I was committed to spending time in hell on earth which in fact was even worse than the hellish life I had actually been living.

With so much time on my hands, my thoughts and feelings of despair forced me to reflect on my actions. I desperately needed to understand and figure out how the heck I had got myself into such a sorry place in my life. I was 32 and felt that I should have been more accomplished. Everyone else my age seemed to have their lives figured out. They were doing grown-up things like having kids and going to dinner parties, meanwhile, I was still dancing on tables, drinking wine straight from the bottle and getting dumped!

There was no doubt about it, I was in serious trouble emotionally and had reached my tipping point. I had enough of everything, especially myself and the miserable, pathetic, shallow life I was sleep-walking through. I had no purpose in the world and was totally unfulfilled. For years I had been berating myself, insisting that I must do better, stop messing around and grow up. Periodically I would be "good" and a model citizen. Then I would go mad, party hard, do something crazy, blow all my good intentions out of the water and end up having yet another lecture of disappointment with myself.

Deep down, I had a niggling feeling what the real problem was. Basically, I was utterly ashamed of myself and had never felt good enough. My head was wrecked from continually listening to my own harsh criticism. People often talk of fighting their demons, but in hindsight, I spectacularly lost the battle with mine and the enemy had drowned "me" in a pool of misery. No matter how hard I tried I couldn't stop judging myself, self-depreciating and comparing myself to others. In my view, everyone was fabulous, and I was worthless. Habitually I filled my head with a cocktail of poisonous thoughts that only drove me more and more demented.

In hindsight, all those thoughts and feelings, particularly the ones about not being good enough, were not anything new. All through my life, even as a child, I never felt "right" in myself. I always had a deep sense that I was different to everyone else and subsequently spent most of my life doing everything I possibly could to hide and suppress my true self. I was a fake who tried desperately to "fit in" to society's expectations (and the ones in my own head) of a middle-class woman in her thirties. I thought I "should" be married, settled down and behave appropriately for my age. Yet no matter how hard I tried I couldn't make myself fit into a different mould. Instead, I had driven myself crazy trying to be someone I was never meant to be and became a misfit in my own life.

As I sat alone and quiet that day, I was terrified of what would happen next. I wished the ground would open up and swallow me there and then so that I wouldn't have to deal with any of it. I was beyond embarrassed by what I had done and where I had ended up. I was also worried sick about the truckload of gossip that I had created and what people were saying about me outside of those four walls.

Looking around the dreary hellhole of "help," my fear turned to blind panic. I was racking my brains for solutions as to how I could make amends and sort my shit out! My mind kept coming back the elephant in the room, the one that was glaringly obvious yet which I had somehow managed to ignore for decades. I simply didn't like myself at all. I had heard of self-love and self-worth, but I didn't understand what those phrases meant. Whenever I heard people talking about those subjects I just assumed they were bonkers. Yet when I thought about how I felt towards myself I could see that hating my body, not appreciating my mind and feeling like I had no redeeming qualities at all, were the biggest and most urgent issues that I needed to overcome. On top of all that, I didn't even like looking at myself in the mirror because I had always been an ugly duckling. I was so small, had straight, dull, brown hair and blue eyes, and was nothing special to look at. I had to learn to like myself, just a little bit would do. Unfortunately, I didn't have a clue where to begin.

I wondered if I could start small and accept myself just as I was. Try to embrace my uniqueness, blemishes and many quirks. If I was going to move my life forward then I absolutely would have to work towards finding love, forgiveness and compassion for myself. I was an expert at putting myself down and making my life a misery but in hindsight that hadn't exactly worked out for me. It was about time I tried a different approach and cut myself some slack.

Even though I was completely lost and broken I was willing to own my mess and do something about it. I had created it and I was going to take responsibility for it. Being in that "garden" was awful and yet it was the intervention and shock to my system that I very much needed. I didn't like being in there, it was scary. Deep down, I knew I was better than that and had let myself down, badly.

When I let myself cry, sob my heart out and fall apart properly in that garden I knew that things were going to change, somehow! They had to, I never wanted to feel so heartbroken ever again. I cried a river that day. Years of torment flooded my eyes and when they stopped, anger replaced them. I wanted to scream my head off and let go of the years of frustration that were pent up inside me. If I could have, I would have punched a hole in the wall and run for the hills.

While it was extremely traumatic to be there, my heart and mind cracked open. I saw clearly how I had continuously hurt myself and vowed that from that day forward I was going on a mission to find my passion and purpose in life. Most certainly, I was going to stop being a fake. I didn't need to change, I just had to be myself, the real one, the one that I had tried so hard to hide all my life. I had put myself through ample misery and enough was enough. Firstly though, I had to pick myself up, dust myself off and find the way out of that God-awful place.

Unfortunately, the Doctors had other ideas about my big revelation and plans. I disliked the psychiatrists who patronized me and told me I was a very sick girl. What did they know? They had only just laid eyes on me and didn't know the first thing about me. I felt they were smug and didn't actually care about me. When I told them so, in no uncertain terms, it didn't exactly go down well but it wasn't about them. It was about me. I knew they were wrong. When I argued back with them they told me I was paranoid! I wasn't. Far from it in fact. For the first time in my life, I was listening to my soul, I had clarity and there was no going back. I knew what was best for me and there was no way their "cure" was right for me. My stubborn streak took over and I promised myself that come hell or high water, I was going to prove them wrong.

I wasn't clinically depressed or clinically anything. They didn't understand that I was living a shit life. I had no self-worth, zero self-esteem, was beyond miserable and was walking in the wrong shoes. I had been clipping my wings all my life to fit into a box that was never meant for me.

I was never going to find what I needed behind those four walls. My recovery and future required me to run as fast as I could and as far away from the life I was living and never ever return to it.

While the doctors didn't agree with me I didn't care in the slightest and checked myself out. When the door finally opened for my big exit, like a butterfly emerging from her cocoon, I flew out of that place and never, ever looked back. The time had come for me to spread my wings wide open and show the world my true colours. I was ready to soar through the clouds, fly high and go places.

My first self-assigned task was to be brave. I needed to get honest with myself and find out what I was made of and decide where my life was going. I also had to introduce my "true" self to the world and most importantly, to me. The "self" who loves to be a bit of a hippy with green fingers and enjoys talking to animals at every opportunity. I needed to let the girl with an unwavering strength of character, buckets of ambition, drive and passion step into the light and be seen.

There was no way I was ever going back to being a caterpillar. That was the end of an era. No longer would I clip my wings to make others feel comfortable, to hell with that. My life was going to be something to write about!

Even though I slammed that chapter closed it was necessary to live through it. All my choices, dreams and achievements are because of my past, it has made me who I am today. Fortunately, after every ending, there is always a brand-new beginning.

Chapter 3
A whole new life
2006

I was free! I began to channel every last ounce of energy, good and bad, into building a whole new life for myself. I started with the easy things such as my job and my lifestyle. I had worked in catering for years and hated absolutely every minute of it. I was done with customers complaining about their food, being obnoxious and treating me like a servant. Whilst I forced myself to smile and sort out their grievances, secretly, I was imagining what it would feel like to pour soup over their head! It was definitely time to move on from hospitality.

Luckily, even though I was feeling like rubbish and ended up behind four walls I somehow managed to work full time and study part time for a Diploma in Physical Therapy, applied anatomy and physiology. When I came home from the "hospital" there was a letter waiting for me. It was good news; after three long years, I had passed all my exams with flying colours. To be honest, I don't know how; I was hungover or still mildly drunk for most of my exams. I even went to an early morning practical test straight from a night-club. But stranger things have happened and in fairness, I have a good memory. I may not always have understood what I was being examined on, but I could regurgitate paragraphs from textbooks which clearly did the trick.

Even though I had a brand-new diploma, I wasn't proud of my achievement. It didn't inspire or drive me in any way. I wanted to be something else. All my life I wanted to be a fitness instructor but had never got around to it.

Growing up, I adored Jane Fonda and her amazing leotards: she was my inspiration. I loved following her workout videos in my bedroom on my VHS player. I jumped around to her aerobic routines and hung on to her every word. She was so fit and nimble. I loved her big 1980s hairstyle and how it bounced up and down during the class. All my life I wanted to look like her, in fact, I just wanted to be her! She was the picture of health, beauty and perfection in my eyes.

At the grand old age of 33, I duly completed a six-month course and became a qualified fitness instructor. While I would always be me and not Jane, I was thrilled to be just a little like my hero.

On the course, I met people who were living a much healthier lifestyle than me (not hard) and I liked what they were teaching me. Suddenly I was interested in nutrition; I learnt about good fats versus bad fats and what a carbohydrate was. As much as I hated hearing it, none of them drank alcohol. I didn't think much of it at the time but the people in my class were a good influence on me. While I thought they were mad not to drink, unbeknownst to me, in some small corner of my mind I was subconsciously starting to think about my own health and liquid consumption.

While I was busy changing my career and learning new skills, I really felt like I needed time out from life in Ireland. I had always loved travelling; it was probably my only one true passion. In my early 20s I went to Australia on a yearlong work visa and had backpacked through southeast Asia. I loved the freedom and fun I had back then and was craving time out. I felt the best thing that I could do was put some distance (a lot) between myself, my current life and the people who knew the old me. I was well aware of the gossip that surrounded me and while I tried to hold my head up high and get on with life, it was hard not to be ashamed.

I applied to work on a cruise ship. Sailing the high seas seemed like the perfect way to get away from everyone and start over, not just in my new career but in life. I was secure in the knowledge that no one would know me or anything about me. Not my past, present or future. If I could get on board I would be free to be "me" without any judgment. I needed to live a little too, I intended on having lots of fun while seeing new parts of the world. As far as I could see it would be a win-win for me. I could sail away, off into the sunset and forget about my recent past.

Even though I was accepted it took some time, 10 months in fact, between the job interview and going to London for my onboard training. While I have always hated winter and dreaded the darkness, I was glad that the wheels were in motion and my life was moving in a whole new direction. For the first time in forever, I had something to look forward to and life didn't feel like such a burden anymore. I was starting to feel excited and had a little hope. At night, as I lay in bed I tried to imagine all the fantastic, exotic places I might be lucky enough to visit.

Finally, January 2007 arrived, and the time came for me to depart for London. I needed to attend a "ship life training camp." From there I would be posted to a liner somewhere in the world. I was relieved to finally be going away. The knot I had been carrying in my stomach started to dissipate just a little. It was the start of a new adventure, not just physically, I was going off to be myself. I might even "find myself" as they say in the movies. Sure I was nervous and apprehensive about what lay ahead but the excitement of walking into the unknown far outweighed my fears. I was going to ride the waves and let the tide take me wherever it wanted

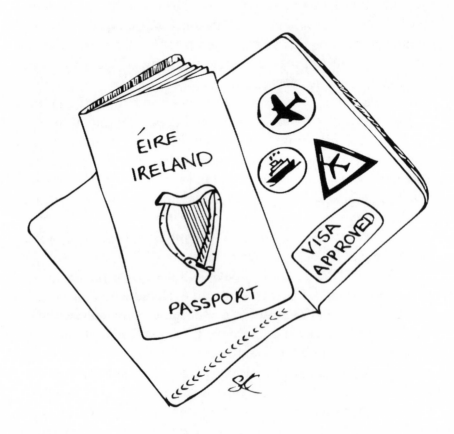

Chapter 4
Passport passion
1970's

My love of adventure and travelling this world was no accident. It's in my DNA thanks to my father. He insisted that we went abroad on our annual family holidays, and I was more than happy to do as I was told back then!

Not many people in the 1970's in Ireland got to go abroad on their summer holidays. The country was poor by anyone's standards. Fuel strikes and ridiculously high interest rates were the norms. Even though Ireland joined the EEC the year I was born (1973), it was still expected that after graduation from school or college young adults would emigrate.

However, when I was four years old and had no idea of the economic or political state of my country, life was good. I had lots of toys, but the best thing was, I was named on my dad's passport. Listed under my big brother's and sister's names on the back page, written clearly in pen, was my full name. I existed on paper and was free to travel.

My very first trip abroad was when I was just 4 years of age. We went to the Canary Islands on an airplane. I have no recollection of the flight but our time on the island was memorable in more ways than one.

Unfortunately, I had an accident in the swimming pool. I was floating along when I slipped through the centre of my inflatable ring. I was so small, even for my age, that my life-saving device offered me no protection whatsoever. Helplessly I got drawn downwards towards the bottom of the pool. I could see other people's legs splashing about while my arms were flapping to no avail. I was sinking like a stone. My mousey brown hair curled awkwardly around my face as large bubbles of air floated from my mouth. As much as I tried I couldn't get back up to the surface.

Thankfully a gentleman who was close by had noticed me slipping through the ring and kindly rescued me. I remember being dragged out of the water. I was coughing profusely while choking and gasping for air as he pulled me from the depths of the pool and pushed me up onto the concrete.

There was some hustle, bustle and crowding around me while I tried to catch my breath. My chest was heaving, and my throat was sore from gagging on the chlorine in the water. I wasn't sure If I was going to throw up or not! When I was finally breathing normally again I was made to sit on a sun lounger, wrapped up in a beach towel at the side of the pool. I must have been in a state of shock as I was shaking like a leaf. Except it wasn't called a shock back then. That didn't exist for kids in the 1970s, it was called, "you're grand, stop crying!"

Scared by my trip to the bottom of the pool, I feared the water for years to come which was probably not helped by the release of the movie Jaws around the same time!

As bad as my nearly drowning incident was, it was not enough to put me off foreign travel. How could it? The sun was shining, it was warm and there was ice cream. I loved being on holiday. I felt warm and happy in my new sandals and Jungle Book t-shirt which weren't hand-me-downs from my sister. They were mine, bought especially for the trip, and I adored them. The three of us kids lined up for photos and said "cheese" which immortalized our first family holiday.

When you're tiny like I was, everything was so big. I couldn't get over the height of the palm trees; they reached up to touch the cloudless sky. They were tall and mighty with a big plume of frizzy leaves at the top. Likewise, I saw what I thought was the entire ocean stretching the whole way to the horizon. Glistening in the sun, the sea was sparkling, twinkling with the movement of the tides making it shimmer under the clear blue sky.

As if the accident in the swimming pool wasn't enough excitement for our first trip abroad, my brother got a horrific sunburn. His pasty Irish skin sizzled in the sun. I have no idea if we had sun cream back then but if we did, it clearly didn't work. The blisters formed into an unsightly layer of bubble wrap which continuously wept goo down his back. I remember him walking around our apartment with his top off. He was in agony. My dad carefully squirted shaving foam in peaks onto the open wounds. The peaks were so high they almost reached my brother's ears before quickly melting from the heat of his burnt skin. We really were the epitome of "idiots abroad," complete novices. Looking back we were the perfect example of how not to holiday in the sun. Mind you, we all have to start somewhere.

Even though I nearly drowned, and my brother returned home missing multiple layers of skin, it was not enough to deter our parents from bringing us on an annual trip abroad. Perhaps they were gluttons for punishment? I prefer to think that we as a family had tenacity and an unbreakable sense of adventure.

I loved travelling with my family. It was the highlight of the year for me. We would pack our bags and lock the front door, the five of us ready for our next adventure. Spending quality time with my parents while going somewhere new was wonderful. I loved it for the change of pace. My parents weren't pushing us out the door to go to school, there was no rushing around and being given out to. Instead, there was sun, sandcastles and hamburgers. We also got to go on a ferry or an airplane. Best of all, whenever we arrived somewhere new my dad waved his passport at the person sitting in the box who would look down and count the three of us. Invariably the immigration officer would pronounce my name all wrong and everyone, except me, would roll around the place laughing. I was annoyed at having a name that no one could pronounce correctly but being let into a new country and seeing the new stamps in dad's passport always made up for the faux-pas.

The following year when I was 5 we took our car to France on the ferry. We were green with nausea and were unable to eat anything for the entire voyage. I remember my poor sister hanging over the side of the ship along with half of the passengers on board; they were all throwing their guts up. For the entire journey, the ship rolled and swayed side to side while endless amounts of crockery and glasses smashed on the floor.

When we finally arrived on dry land we were worse for wear, but we still managed to drive to beautiful Paris. It was a dream come true to see the Eiffel Tower and the Mona Lisa. Paris was so glamorous to me; it was the height of sophistication. We even got to spend an hour driving around the Arc De Triomphe because dad couldn't get into the outer lane to make an exit!

While we were in France I played on the beaches of Normandy and got dragged around some World War bunkers which, when you're five years old, are not very exciting at all. To me, they were just great big concrete sheds with not very imaginative graffiti sprayed on them.

Instead, for me the highlight of the trip was learning some French words. "Pommes Frites" was top of my list for saying in my best French accent. I also managed to learn how to count to three. I played with "funny money", and we drove on the "wrong side" of the road. It was so exciting, new and different. I was shown that there was a great big world outside of Ireland and I wanted to discover every last bit of it. That was when my love of other cultures, languages and the world began. I loved the sights and smells that every new town had to offer. People were different everywhere we went; they had really strong accents and they could not understand us in the slightest. Even when dad raised his voice and repeated himself, they still looked blankly at him! They also had strange cultures like kissing each other on the cheek and eating weird things such as frogs' legs, snails and foie gras which were all vile to a five-year-old. I still have memories of walking around the fish markets and seeing lobsters swimming in tanks with elastic bands on their hands. Curiously, I banged on the aquarium window and tried to talk to the molluscs. "Bonjour!"

My mother used a crochet needle to extract a snail which looked like a gigantic snot from its shell. I nearly vomited as she swallowed it whole. While I have been back to France on numerous occasions as an adult I have never once felt the need to delve into the world of escargots!

We returned to France the following summer for more pommes frites and then we hit the big time. We went transatlantic. Was I spoiled? You bet I was.

Getting on the jumbo jet was a turning point in my young life. In a few hours, we were on another continent, way over on the other side of the world. We landed in Orlando, Florida. The sunshine state, home of Disney and theme parks so big they took days to walk around. It was another world; everything was bigger and better. Even my excitement reached a whole new level, it was off the Richter scale. I never thought that such an incredible place could exist.

At Universal Studios, I went on roller coasters which were fast and furious. I had to stand on my tippy toes to meet the height restrictions and then nearly fell out of the fast-moving carriage as I was too small for the safety harness. I didn't care in the slightest. It just made me want to do more and more crazy rides. I loved the feeling of speed and fear rolled into one, I couldn't get enough of it and instantly became an adrenaline junkie!

Disney World in Florida was a dream come true for me and my big sister. We were greeted by Cinderella's Castle in the Magic Kingdom. I was bowled over by the colours, vibrancy and sheer scale of the theme park. Everything about the place was magical. It was a living fairy tale with our most loved Disney characters walking around for us to meet. However, for me, it was the fast-moving runaway train and the vomit-inducing spinning teacups that were the best fun. We went on them numerous times because they were just so thrilling. All five of us screamed our heads off and laughed hysterically as we were thrown around on both of those rides. We had the time of our lives.

Our number one favourite ride was "It's a small world." The five of us were piled into a little boat as we gently sailed through shallow waters listening to the most repetitive and annoying song in the world! However it worked, it seeped into my head and forever lodged itself in there. I can still close my eyes to this day, sing the tune in my head and I am transported back to 7-year-old me on that ride.

Every country on the planet was represented by dolls dancing in their national costume. The French dolls were dancing the can-can beside a great big Eiffel tower. Little Japanese dolls dressed in geisha clothes held their hands in a prayer position and gently bowed their heads as we sailed on by. We whooped and hollered when we came to Ireland. We were over the moon and thrilled to see the little Irish dolls looking so happy. They were wearing bright green dresses, had electric orange hair, and were surrounded by leprechauns, rainbows and pots of gold. They danced with glee, giving it socks, kicking their legs furiously as they bobbed up and down with gusto. Just like the other countries the Irish dolls were smiling and making their country proud.

It was the most amazing thing I had ever seen. I had no idea of the word stereotypical back then and even if I did, I wouldn't have cared. I was in my element, touring the world and picking out places that I absolutely had to visit in the future. If I didn't like a particular doll's outfit I wouldn't put that country on my to-do list.

Looking back now, I can see that the ride was teaching me to be accepting of different cultures and to see how we are all sharing one world. Being so young and impressionable it was the perfect time to be brought on a whistle-stop tour of the earth and introduced to its many nationalities. After that theme park ride, more than anything I wanted to circumnavigate the world. I couldn't wait to meet people from other cultures, see famous landmarks and colourful outfits for real. I vowed to myself that when I grew up I would be a globetrotter. My childhood dreams were set in stone. The only thing I needed to do was to find a way.

The air hostesses seemed so glamorous on our long-haul flight; it made me think that perhaps I could be one when I grew up. I didn't like their uniform much or how their hair was scraped back into a severe bun, but I was willing to suck it up if it meant I could go to Disney World again. However, while I matured in years I was left pint-sized and never made the height requirements that were imposed back then to be cabin crew.

Years later when physical measurements had been abolished I applied to Emirates Airlines. How glamorous! I would get to live in Dubai with all expenses paid and fly all over the world as they had a very comprehensive network. My earnings would be tax-free too. My plan was to send home all my money and buy a mansion. It really was a dream job for me.

The only problem was they turned me down. I got as far as a second interview and that was that. We had to play games to display initiative and teamwork. As a small group, we had to silently build a square with oddly shaped pieces to show we could figure things out and work with others. I showed initiative all right, I took all the parts and assembled them into the final product in double quick time. There was no need for anyone to get involved, I had it sorted! Besides the other girls in the group had spent the first five minutes faffing around and had the pieces upside down, they were getting nowhere. It was painful to watch them, it was so obvious to me how the pieces fitted together. Thank goodness I was there to take full control of the situation and show everyone how to do it right. They would have been there forever if it had not been for me!

I learnt a very valuable lesson that day. Some people, i.e. me, are better off being self-employed and making up their own rules as they go along. There really is no "I" in a team, especially not an "I" like me.

When we were not on family holidays my father worked hard on our farm. He put in long arduous hours all year round while my poor mother had the pleasure of us three running riot. While we didn't see that much of him during the week I always looked forward to Sunday evenings when we would watch the long-range weather forecast together. I loved spending time with him. He was always telling me to watch out and see what the high pressure over the Atlantic Ocean was doing. We needed it to move a bit more north and push the low pressure that sat over Ireland out of the way. If it did it would help the crops to grow and bring nice weather with it. After all, dad had to harvest and simultaneously look after the pigs. He was always predicting how harsh the winter would be based on the number of berries on the trees, how quickly the grass was growing or which way the birds sat facing on the fence! I don't know if he was ever right, but I like to think that he was in tune with mother nature.

Because of him, I loved to muck around on the farm and help him dig holes. I also loved to climb trees and swing out of everything that would hold me. In general, I was a tomboy and was happy to be one. I didn't care for dresses or dolls. I much preferred to do cartwheels and run around the fields. While dad got annoyed with us for playing with the bales of hay, he instilled in me a huge respect for mother nature and all creatures great and small. Our farm was filled with cattle and pigs, but we also had endless visits from pheasants, rabbits, field mice and deer. We always had cats and dogs too. In our home: animals were just par for the course.

My father's knowledge of and interest in nature fuelled a desire in me to go to exotic locations and see their wildlife. I would lie on the floor flicking through the pages of my favourite book, the atlas. I wanted to know where everywhere was and how I could get there. One year my granddad bought me the best atlas ever. It was full of facts and figures about each and every country. It had glossy colourful pictures of volcanos,524 birds and rivers too. It was the best present ever. I was in my element when I had my head stuck in that book. I would lose track of time and in my mind, I was exploring the most exotic places on the planet.

When our very modern A- Z encyclopaedias arrived I had everything in the world at my fingertips. The World Wide Web did not exist back then - we would have to wait until 1989 for that! Instead, we had books that told us everything we needed to know about anything and everything on the planet. The whole world was accessible to me and while I was never much of a reader, I loved looking at pictures of fabulous places and learning about everything under the sun. I was able to look up all kinds of things I had never heard of. It was mind-blowing to me at such a young age to think that there was so much out in the world for me to do and see.

I was well and truly infected with a travel bug: there was nothing else I wanted to do. If I couldn't work for the airlines then there were always boats. Not the ferry that I had gone to France on, no, I wanted to work on luxury liners as glamorous as the Titanic (before she sank.) The Sunday newspaper which my parents bought every week always had an advert in the classifieds looking for crew to work on luxury cruise ships. Every Sunday I sat and stared at that advertisement. I tried to memorise the details because I knew I'd be killed if I took the scissors to the paper! The sports news was on the back of the advert, and we had to see what Ollie Campbell and the rest of the Irish rugby team were up to back then.

I never forgot that advertisement or my dreams of travelling far and wide. That was the reason I applied to the cruise ships for my much-needed time out. All along, all through my formative years, I knew what I wanted to do. I had just forgotten somewhere along the way.

However, that was about to change. On day 10 of my cruise ship training in London, the senior instructor walked into the classroom and called my name. He had a white envelope in his hand. Butterflies in my stomach started doing back flips, my palms went clammy, and I couldn't speak. This was it. The moment I had been waiting all my life for. It was my posting details. He handed me the envelope and winked.

"Life is either a great adventure or nothing."

-Helen Keller

Chapter 5
Ahoy there matey!
Singapore 2007

After a long flight from Heathrow, I touched down in Singapore to meet my cruise ship. I was sent to work on a super-expensive luxury ship that was setting sail to voyage around the world. I could not have picked a better boat for myself. The itinerary was out of this world; to name a few stops, I was going to Japan, Korea, China, Australia and New Zealand. Even better, I wouldn't have to endure any winter days as the ship was following sunshine and summer in the southern hemisphere.

When the taxi pulled up at the harbour and I caught my first glimpse of the liner I gasped. It was magnificent. Floating in the water was a whiter-than-white ship that gleamed in the sunshine. She was beautiful and just as I had imagined. She was my very own Titanic, and I was going to call her home for the next year. As I walked up the gangplank I was shaking with equal measures of nerves and excitement, but I knew I was where I was meant to be. Looking up at the huge liner I had definitely made the right decision to leave Ireland.

There was hustle and bustle around the entrance door as security was busy x-raying everyone's luggage. Sheepishly, I announced my arrival to the first officer I saw who was checking passports. He looked very dashing in his white uniform which had numerous gold stripes on the shoulders. I had never actually thought about that, sailors and uniforms! How amazing was it that all the crewmen were dressed as if they were in the movie *An Officer and a Gentleman*. As if by magic my new home suddenly became even more magnificent.

After some paperwork, I was officially a crew member. I even had a Seaman's Book to prove it. I was the ship's brand-new fitness instructor reporting for duty.

Even though I was qualified there was one small problem. I had never actually taught a fitness class to real, paying customers. Sure, I had practised with my classmates, but we didn't care if we made mistakes, or if the class was rubbish. We just needed each other to pass our exams and get our papers. It suddenly dawned on me that I would be expected to motivate and inspire passengers to work out and step away from the food buffets.

That wasn't my only problem. At that time I was still very partial to smoking and drinking alcohol. Even though I loved doing aerobics and weight training I wasn't exactly a beacon of health.

Nonetheless, in between cigarette breaks, I exercised my way around the world on the high seas. I taught aerobics badly, but thankfully no one seemed to notice! Luckily the guests were only on-board for 2- 3 weeks at a time which meant all I had to do was rehash the same routine over and over and over again. I also pretended to be a Yoga guru. I had been given a Yoga crash course during my onboard cruise ship training week in London, but it was about as much use as ice to Eskimos. Luckily I had the initiative to buy Yoga books and DVDs in London before departure. Every day while in my cabin I frantically read up on Yoga poses and did my best to follow along with the lady in my DVDs. Thanks to my excellent memory skills, I memorised her "moves" and parroted her words back to my class. I faked it for the first few months for sure. There was nothing else I could do, it was sink or swim, literally. However, to be fair to myself, once I got into my rhythm, bought a few more Yoga books along the voyage and did a lot of studying I was as good as any "real" teacher.

I absolutely loved my time on the ship. I made friends with so many people that I would never have otherwise met. We were all so different, but we all worked together to keep the ship afloat. Naturally, it wasn't all work: below deck, the fun and crew life was infamous! At times I partied hard and got hauled into the staff officer for urine tests. There was strict protocol about crew drinking but somehow, miraculously, I never failed a test. We had parties, table tennis competitions, quiz nights and calendar events. I loved being part of one big happy colourful family bobbing around the sea. There were a few scandals - sailors are notorious for having a woman in every port but there was onboard action too! I even had a romance or two of my own. It was a wonderful, liberating time in my life and I made the most of being a free spirit in exotic locations.

Those twelve months were so much fun. It was exactly what I needed. Being away "from everything" gave me a chance to be free from my recent past and the gossip that went with it. It was the perfect opportunity for me to live it up, be carefree, start to accept myself fully and live my life by my rules. I got to see so many places that I had read about as a child in my atlas. I docked in 40 countries during that time. We visited some incredibly amazing places for a few hours and sometimes a little longer. I spent a day in Brunei, I wandered around the streets of Taipei in Taiwan. I smelt frankincense in Oman and ate an authentic curry in India. We even docked in Odesa in Ukraine and then sailed to Sochi in Russia. To be honest, I didn't like the Black Sea much: I much preferred the ports in the Mediterranean that we docked in. The Med was much more vibrant and colourful. Sorrento was my favourite. It was very upmarket with exclusive hotels perched on the cliffs overlooking the sea. I kept waiting for James Bond to pull up beside me in his Aston Martin and whisk me away but alas...

The world was my oyster. I loved my work and lifestyle on board the cruise ship. I was happy, having fun and seeing the world for free. I also made a wonderful, lifelong friend while on the cruise. Linh was so funny and happy. She oozed sunshine and vitality, much like Florida, in the USA where she was from. She was very clued into her self-worth and self-esteem, loved tarot cards and all things a bit "out there." We were drawn to each other and had endless discussions about life, love and finding our purpose. She opened up my eyes to books and speakers that would help me on my quest for self-discovery and inner happiness. She was like my very own personal mentor who took me under her wing and guided me to scratch the surface of my soul. She pushed me gently and gave me the courage to look inside. She was a breath of fresh air and my introduction to personal development. I was able to talk openly with her about all sorts of "hippy dippy" stuff and never once felt stupid or judged. I loved it when she would break out her tarot cards and do a reading for me. I lapped up all her advice on matters of the heart and the head. She was the wisest and most fulfilled person I had ever met.

It was an incredible time in my life and one that I will never forget. It was the perfect trip to reignite my lust for adventures, exotic travels and the big wide world. While I got bite-sized tastes of some countries, which was great, I was disappointed that there was never enough time to get immersed properly. As a result, whenever I visit a new place now, I ensure I have more time to sightsee, immerse myself in their culture and endeavour to see everything I can.

While I was beyond happy during that time it was not "real life." My world tour was exactly what I needed after my "troubles." I was starting to accept and openly be myself. I was reading everything that Linh gave me and more. I was living life the way I wanted to and had finally achieved the "globetrotter" status that I had always dreamed of. However, the day came when I knew that it was time to return to Ireland, face reality and build a new career and life for myself. Saying goodbye to ship life was hard but I was ready to plant my feet back on solid ground.

One thing I was certain of - there was no way I was going back home to Ireland to work Monday to Friday 9-5 pm and have someone dictate to me how much time off I could have. No way. I planned to work for myself and make my own rules. I wanted to work hard and build a great business in the wellness industry that would allow me plenty of time off on my terms. I promised myself that no matter what, I would always find the time and money to explore, travel, learn and meet others. I also vowed that I would never let life get on top of me again. With the help of Linh and her books, I worked on coping mechanisms and was able to face any difficulties that came my way. After all, there was a great big world out there and none of my problems were unsolvable. In fact, while they were problems to me, in the grand scheme of life, they were first-world problems. There are so many people on the planet who would have loved to be in my shoes and have my "issues." Travelling the globe on the ship opened my eyes to how the other half lives. I realised that in reality, I had very little to complain about.

Returning back to Ireland was lovely but there was one thing I had to do before I "settled in." I wanted to become a "real" bona fide Yoga teacher, and there was only one place on the planet that I felt was good enough to train in. India was calling. Even better, Linh was coming too. We were going to qualify together and then go travelling for 3 weeks. I packed my bags once again and headed east for 7 weeks.

Chapter 6
Namaste! Is this a cult?
India 2008

The taxi pulled up outside of the ashram that was going to be home for the next four weeks. The trip from the airport had been a little manic due to the crazy traffic and the way of driving in India. It was not bad. It was just different to the "rules must be obeyed" ways of the west. All bets are off when you are a passenger in India, and I wouldn't have had it any other way. India was exhilarating, hectic and colourful, all at the same time. It was unique, beautiful and bonkers which could explain why I loved it so much. While I had been on many day trips to India whilst on the cruise ship this was going to be my first full immersion there.

I loved everything about the country, though I must admit it does take some getting used to. As you might expect, there were hordes of people, and everyone was frantically going somewhere. The traffic was mental, and beeping the horn appeared to be a compulsory sport. Yet it all worked.

India was a feast for the senses and my personal favourite was the smell. India had a very noticeable and distinct fragrance that wafted through the air no matter where I was. It was pungent with a sort of sweet, yet musky nose. I could never quite make out what exactly the base odours were, but I know that in its perfume there was definitely turmeric, cumin, all kinds of incense sticks and air pollution. The smell still lingers in my senses, it is as if it can never be un-smelt!

India was vividly colourful too. Walls and shrines were painted in bold pinks, deep greens, bright oranges, blood reds and cornflower blues. They were not subtle in any way; quite the opposite, there was no chance of missing the highly decorative wall art.

Everywhere in India there were wonderful Hindu statues standing high on altars decorated with countless fresh flowers. The various deities received fresh flower garland necklaces daily from their worshippers as offerings. The ones made from bright orange marigolds were my favourite. Now, whenever I close my eyes and think of India, it is not the poverty and overcrowding I see in my memories. It is the bright orange marigolds that soothed the atmosphere while bringing tranquillity and vibrancy to the entire land.

We finally arrived, just about in one piece, to our lodgings thanks to our rally driver in the front seat. Our Ashram was nestled in a tropical corner in the east of Kerala, south India. Linh had found it online and I was happy to go along with her choice. I couldn't believe how quiet and remote it was. I never imagined that there was anywhere peaceful in India but much to my delight, she had found an oasis that the one billion local souls hadn't!

I had come for one reason and one reason only; I was on a mission to get my Yoga qualification so that I could get my insurance in Ireland and teach legally. That was it. I didn't want any frills or optional extras. I especially didn't want any mumbo jumbo or too much hippy crap! I just wanted to get the job done as efficiently as possible, get my certificate, tick the box and go travelling.

Before we entered the gates of the Ashram I needed to do something special. I was going to have my last cigarette before I entered the complex. I had made the decision that this would be the perfect time to quit and try to become pure. After all, it wouldn't be very Yoga-like for me to smoke. I was embarking on my new wellness expedition, and I needed to lead by example if I was going to be a good teacher. I tried to savour it and enjoy my last moments as a smoker, but Linh was shouting at me to hurry up. She was being eaten by mosquitos and I had the repellent in my bag.

An ashram is like a little community, a safe haven of tranquillity and serenity. It is a place where people go to find peace, detox and meditate. I didn't know that though! I thought I was going to a hardcore Yoga teacher training bootcamp and wasn't expecting what I found.

I didn't mind having to hand over my phone; it was pre-smartphone days so that was no big deal. Besides, there was no wi-fi and WhatsApp wasn't even invented back then. I had my little compact camera and was happy with that.

As we walked through the grounds to our room I noticed that there were a lot of people sitting around under trees. They all looked deep in contemplation as though they were transfixed on something. I was sure they must have had earphones on and were listening to something very important. It was the only possible explanation as far as I could see.

While our lodgings were basic they were absolutely fine. I was never precious about things like that. We each had a bed, a mosquito net and a little table to share. The showers and toilets were communal, but we didn't mind in the slightest. Less water in our room meant fewer insects to bite us.

The grounds of the estate were lovely. They were lush and tropical with plenty of shady spots to escape the heat. I liked it there; there was a nice breeze that rustled through the tropical plants, and it was very quiet. I could hear the birds chirping in the trees along with plenty of buzzing from insects. Unfortunately, creepy crawlies loved those tropical plants too. For a person who loves to travel, I am still a bit of a wuss when it comes to spiders. There were plenty of them in Kerala and notably everywhere I went to sit in the Ashram. It was as if they were following me on purpose.

We were given our teacher training uniforms which were extremely unflattering. A shapeless egg yolk yellow t-shirt and baggy white trousers. They were so unflattering, and I can honestly say that not one person on the course looked good in them. Apparently, those colours were chosen because they represent knowledge but all they reminded me of was the Vatican. (I was never much of a fan of the Catholic church even though I was baptised a Catholic.)

Our first morning, and every morning after that, started at 5am. It was the middle of the night as far as I was concerned. There wasn't even a kettle around to make a cup of tea. Each morning in the dark I trudged half asleep to the big hall for Satsang, which was chanting and a philosophical talk with the Swami (a Hindu male religious teacher).

Myself and all the other students (about 150 of us) sat in rows along the concrete floor facing the "altar," where the Swami welcomed us. Then he started chanting which would last for an eternity. One by one, everyone joined in. I couldn't understand it, how did they know what to do and how did everyone except me know the words? They were chanting away with him in perfect harmony. They even had the pronunciation right even though it was in Sanskrit. Most of them had their eyes closed and were in some sort of trance. It was all so over the top; I began to worry and started to have a panic attack. Thoughts were racing through my mind - What the hell was going on? Where the heck was I? Had I walked into a cult? As far as I could see they were all headbangers and I needed to find the exit door fast.

As if that wasn't bad enough after the chanting came the singing. Tambourines and drums were being handed out to the very enthusiastic audience. Dear God! It was a full-blown hippy, pot-bashing party. People were swaying side to side, wiggling their bums on the cold concrete while their singing got louder and louder. The tambourines were in full force, which was bad enough, but they were completely out of sync with the tune. It was really annoying me. I couldn't understand how they could all be tone-deaf and not realise what a travesty they were committing.

I looked at Linh to see if she was as bewildered as me, but she was in her element. She was as bad as the others and was giving it socks too. How did she know the words? I was mortified for them all, scarlet in fact. What were they at? Looking around I couldn't find anyone else like me who was in full submarine mode. I had my periscope up in the hopes to find some "normality" in the crowd. It didn't appear there was any. I was the only beacon of hope in a hall full of weirdos!

After two hours of Satsang, we were handed bowls of dried bananas before we began two hours of rigorous Yoga (asanas). The first time I saw the small bowls I just assumed there was one for everyone in the audience. There wasn't. When we were told to take just four pieces each and pass the bowl on to our classmates I nearly died. I was starving. We had endured two hours of a hippy festival in the middle of the night which was being topped off by food rationing.

After two hours of rigorous Yoga, I was ready to eat my own arm. I felt malnourished and wanted to call the Red Cross to come and rescue me. Everyone else was happy and didn't seem to notice that they were expected to live off of fresh air. I couldn't understand how they were all so calm and joyful. I was beyond hungry, and my irritability was ready to erupt like a volcano! In hindsight, I was not coping well at all with the life lessons I was being taught. (Patience, self-control, abstinence and humility.) My internal dialogue (ego), was once again on a runaway train. I just didn't know it at the time.

Every day was the same routine. We had our main meal of the day at 10am which considering we had been up for five hours already was more than welcome. It was mandatory to eat in silence so that we could be in the moment and savour our food. I had no problem with that; I was so busy stuffing my face and trying to eat as much food as I could that I didn't have time for inane small talk. (The food was really good though; it was so fresh and vegan too.)

After "breakfast/ dinner" we had a little break. Twenty minutes of free time for self-care and personal hygiene. Thank goodness I hadn't actually finished my packet of cigarettes. For the first few days I snuck out of the grounds and had a sneaky ciggie down by the river. Puffing away by the water I felt "normal" and free for just a few minutes. My little daily adventures gave me a chance to reflect on the madness of the morning ritual that I had been subjected to. I would have run away except that I needed my qualification to get insurance in Ireland. I kept telling myself to just grin and bear it. I had to constantly remind myself to stop being so annoyed with my classmates. If they wanted to bang drums it was really no big deal and it didn't make any difference whatsoever to my life. I knew I had to learn to let others live their life their way, stop judging and comparing everyone to me and me to them. Deep down in my heart, I was conscious that if I wanted to be accepted as myself by others then I had to start with my own behaviour. It was just so darn hard though. I had nothing in common with them and even though I was travelling with Linh, I felt alone and isolated from the happy clappers on the inside.

The days rolled by slowly and our routine was the same day in and day out. As well as lessons in philosophy, doing Yoga, being starved to death and shaking tambourines we each had a job to fulfil our Karma Yoga. Mine was to sweep and mop the floors in the hallway. I liked doing that. Not only was it physical and helped me to burn off some "crazy" but it was relaxing too. Swishing the mop back and forth I enjoyed making patterns and shapes on the floors. What appealed to my nature most was that I could see instant results. The floor was dirty one minute and the next it was clean. I could get my head around that.

I also enjoyed the walking meditations we sometimes went on at dawn. All 150 of us trekked down to the lake and sat on the shore. We had to hum and chant as dawn broke but I didn't mind that so much. I never felt self-conscious at all when I was in the great outdoors. I was in my natural habitat and felt close to "mother nature/creation."

It was beautiful to see the sun rising. At first, there was a little crack of light appearing in the dark, as if someone had slashed a black curtain and was trying to peek in with a torch. It was hypnotic to watch that little glimmer of light become bigger and bigger as the torch got brighter and brighter until the darkness was no more. I felt especially renewed and energised on those mornings. Those particular days were special to me, they had meaning and made me feel good about life. Seeing the splendid sunrise radiating yellows and oranges across the sky felt like I was receiving my very own fresh marigold garland to brighten up my life. I was even starting to find a warm fuzzy feeling inside my heart.

Even when we were back inside the ashram to continue our programme I was much more serene on those days. I think in hindsight, my problem with being in the ashram was that it had four high walls. Maybe, just maybe, it subconsciously reminded me too much of the hospital I had run away from.

As time went by, I got more used to the routine and started to settle in. I wouldn't say I was part of the furniture, but I was no longer so eager to find the emergency exit. I did try my best not to escape to the river each day for a cigarette break. Unfortunately, I hadn't learned willpower at that stage in my life. Inevitably I gave in some days, but at least it wasn't every day. On those days I chain-smoked my head off in the few minutes I had free. Much like the main meal of the day I felt it was better to overindulge just in case there was a famine or a cigarette shortage.

You may wonder where I got my cigarette supply from!? We had occasional days off and while we were allowed to leave the ashram a lot of students opted not to. They preferred to stay in the "zone." As I was never in the zone I ran out of the place, hopped in a taxi and went straight to the nearest town. I bought enough cigarette supplies to last me a lifetime. (I had to smuggle them into the ashram. I was able to throw them over the wall and collect them later!) I even had a beer for good measure while I was out and about. Even though I didn't miss alcohol at all it was like I had a devil on my shoulder egging me on to do it. While I indulged it actually wasn't enjoyable in any way. It made me feel worse about myself and upset my stomach too. I was eating a pure Sattvic diet in the Ashram and my body was naturally cleansing itself. Throwing a beer, even just a small one into my newly cleansed gut didn't sit well at all physically or mentally.

After around two weeks I turned a corner and got into the swing of things, just a little bit. I started to read my textbooks and do my homework. While I often had to read a page or an entire chapter a few times to understand what the author was talking about, I got there eventually. I really depended on Linh's help too. She was so good at helping me and took the time to explain the philosophical passages. They were long-drawn-out, frilly and confusing, with parables and stories about this and that. I wished the writers had just written what they meant instead of going around in circles. It would have been much easier for someone like me.

The other students were helpful too. It turned out they weren't as bad as I initially thought. They were actually nice and friendly. When I spoke with some others, I learnt that they were actually a lot like me too. They had little to no understanding of the deeper meaning of life but were willing to learn it at their own pace too. Chatting with them made me feel a little better especially when a few of them admitted to miming the morning chants as they had no idea what the words were supposed to be either. Phew! I wasn't alone after all.

As the weeks rolled by, at 5am Satsang, Linh and I sat with my newfound comrades. One was Canadian and two were British. As a joke, we took the tambourines and drums and joined in with the happy clappers. Much to our amusement, it felt good, we were like our own heavy metal/rock band giving it socks on the instruments. Funnily enough, when I was with them I didn't care that we were out of tune or not matching the beat of the chant. The first few times we played them we were actively taking the p**s out of the proceedings and were in hysterics as we egged each other on. However, after doing that for a few days in a row, something changed. We were enjoying ourselves, for real! It was so much fun to dance, make up our own words to the chants and let loose on the drums. I was like Animal from the Muppet Show. At first I was shy and doing my best to be a professional musician but by the end of the four weeks, I was going ballistic and battering the life out of the poor drum. In fact, I was even more enthusiastic than some of the hard-core happy clappers that I had witnessed on day one.

Even though I was just getting "into it" I wasn't sad when the four weeks ended. Perhaps it was just enough for me at that time. It had felt like penance at the start, but in the long run it was worth it. I got what I went for, I passed my Yoga teacher training and was bona fide. I had cut down on smoking too but was not quite ready to quit. I also lost weight and looked great (if I say so myself) from hours and hours of Yoga. The mirrors in the Ashram weren't great which suited me fine. However, even though they were tarnished and old, I could see that my skin was clear, and my eyes were piercingly blue. I looked so healthy and much to my surprise, I felt happier in myself too.

While I hadn't "got" all the teachings I had understood the importance of being in the moment. I liked mopping the floors and not having any distractions, especially from technology. I loved looking at the lake and watching the gentle ripples dissipate into stillness. Sitting on a bench with the sun on my face during my breaks was my favorite of all. I also learnt that those people I saw on my very first day, the ones who I was sure had earphones on (they didn't) were meditating. Imagine that? I was pleased that in the space of four weeks I had learnt how to do that too. For some reason, I just was better at it when I was near water rather than inside four walls.

With our teacher training certificates in our hands we left the Ashram. Myself and Linh flew up to the north of India for three weeks and explored the area. We went to Delhi and Jaipur and much to my delight, we visited the Taj Mahal. I just had to recreate the iconic photo of Princess Diana from her visit there. I sat on the very same bench as her, in the exact same spot. I even had my body turned to replicate her posture. While I enjoyed duplicating her moment in time there were a lot of differences. There were around a million other people there that day with me. (The Taj isn't exactly a secret location.)I didn't look as glamorous as her but nonetheless, I looked nice in a huge white sun hat. The biggest contrast, which was most notable, was that I wasn't miserable like Princess Diana was in her photo. I was the complete opposite. I looked happy and refreshed, in fact I was glowing. After my trip to the Ashram and travelling around India, I was finally radiating sunshine just like my dear friend Linh

"When she transformed into a butterfly, the caterpillars spoke not of her beauty but of her weirdness. They wanted her to change back into what she had always been. But she had wings."

-Dean Jackson

Chapter 7
Home
Ireland 2008

True to my word, when I returned to Ireland I didn't work 9am to 5pm for someone else. Instead, I set about creating Yoga classes and building a wellness business. Even though it was challenging to start from scratch, I was more than happy to give it a bash. I was doing what I believed in, enjoyed immensely and after working for a year on the ship, I was more than confident that I was good at it too.

While getting my business up and running was arduous there were other difficulties to overcome. I never expected a world economic crash to happen the minute I set foot back in Ireland. It was tough to get the ball rolling, but every cloud has a silver lining. As I had very few customers and was starting from nothing, it didn't impact my earnings or motivation. Not one to waste time, I got more qualifications, Pilates and physiotherapy based, which were great for my resume and area of expertise. However, the highlight of my life, my reason for getting up each day was that I was helping the few customers I had to move and look after their health. I hoped that I could inspire them the same way Jane Fonda had inspired me.

With the help of hypnosis I even stopped smoking which was a huge achievement for me. Finally I was "clean" and didn't feel like a fake health "guru." I was also eating much better and trying to learn as much as I could about nutrition. My body looked and felt amazing from my trip to India thanks to all the fresh food, water and fruit I had been consuming. My body seemed to run better on lentils and vegetables. I had so much energy and felt like I could take on the word. Thanks to that experience, I made the connection between what I was eating and my mood. When my system was overloaded on sugar I felt crap! When I ate well I felt great. It was so simple and yet the link had been totally overlooked by myself and those doctors back in 2005.

Food really was an issue for me. I wasn't coeliac or anything, but I was definitely food sensitive. Certain foods made me sleepy while the more fruit and vegetables I ate the more spring I had in my step. I wanted to continue feeling as good as I had in India and really tried my best to look after my diet. While I had no interest in becoming a dietitian, I hoovered up all the books and YouTube videos I could find on the link between gut health and mental health. There was so much information to consume which confirmed my recent discovery. The saying "you are what eat" and the old wives' tale about "an apple a day" was in fact true.

While I was busy with my new career there was one big part of my life that I needed to face up to since returning home. I had to take care of the shame and embarrassment that I felt whenever I met relations and people "who knew what I had done."

It was never talked about to my face, of course not! It was Ireland after all, we much prefer to talk about people behind their backs. I knew that even though I had made myself disappear for well over a year, when those people met me, they assumed they were dealing with the girl from 2005.

I wasn't her anymore, she had been my fake facade. I had since wished her well and sent her on her way. I was different after travelling all over the world on the ship and spending time in India. I needed to show off the newfound "happy clapper" in me to everyone and let them know that they were in fact dealing with a whole new Sinead who was much nicer. She even knew how to smile.

Even though Linh had returned to the cruise ships, we were in touch. I missed her but was glad that she was following her own path. From afar, she was still mentoring me, recommending books and motivational speakers for me to listen to. I loved reading her emails and felt like she was holding my hand along the way. She gave me the courage to go and "talk to someone." After all, unlike every item of clothing I owned, I hadn't come with a care label. I still didn't know how to mind myself fully by having healthy, protective boundaries.

Over the years I had none and it showed. I was a walkover. Even though people always saw me as feisty I wasn't at all. Sure, I was argumentative, but ultimately, I always gave in to other people's needs and let them have their way. More often than not, much to my detriment, I would end up apologizing for things I hadn't even done. It was just easier to take the blame than to listen to arguments. After a row with someone, I always was the bigger person and put out the olive branch first. While that all sounds very admirable, I was just teaching people that I didn't matter. In fact, I was actually showing others my incredibly low self-worth and the poor standards I had set for myself. As you know, it even got to the point where I believed I didn't matter either. I had to reach out and get help. In order to build boundaries I had to call in the big guns!

I spent hours and hours working on myself by attending seminars and personal development courses. I read even more self-help books and listened to more podcasts from motivational speakers. I searched high and low for answers and went down rabbit holes that always brought me back to the same place. Everything starts and finishes with how you feel about yourself. There was just no getting away from it. How I treated myself, mentally and physically, would determine my inner happiness.

I did some counselling too, but I wasn't able for it. It wasn't easy coming face to face and challenging head-on my deepest, darkest thoughts and emotions. I just wasn't ready to open up and didn't want to talk about my feelings or my childhood. Part of me didn't see the point while the other part was like a crab that ran a mile and retreated deep into the sand. I knew that my feelings of not being good enough and not belonging were exceptionally deep-rooted. I had self-sabotaged over and over because of them. Even after all I had been through I couldn't put myself and my upbringing under scrutiny. Besides, I wanted to move forward and not spend hours in the past. I found a reason every time to cancel my appointments until the therapist quit calling.

However, I didn't give up on my mental health. Far from it. I just chose a different approach. I much preferred the holistic modalities I had learnt in India and continued with meditation, mindfulness and Yoga classes. I discovered journalling and talking out loud to myself were exceptionally helpful too. I was able to process my thoughts and feelings when I could see and hear them. Much to my relief my head was less scrambled as a result.

Due to spending so much time online looking for deep and meaningful answers to life I found other fascinating human behaviours. It turned out that I was exceptionally interested in reading articles on personality types and learning about body language. I couldn't get enough of it. I just loved that what was going on inside of a person's mind was legible on the outside. I wondered how it was that for all those years when I was utterly miserable that no one had spotted my torment through my posture and expressions. In hindsight, people have admitted to me that they just thought I was a moody cow! Someone even used the phrase "anti-Christ," which was fair enough. I just wish that they had asked me why I was miserable instead of accepting my poor behaviour. (N.B. Pain is visible if we choose to see it.)

I also preferred to goal set and look to a brighter future filled with travel and adventure. I wanted to have lots of things to look forward to and places to go. I still had my favourite atlas that my granddad had given me all those years ago and found comfort flicking through it. Even though some countries no longer existed, that was only geography. The world was still out there and waiting for me to visit.

Two years passed by in a flash: it was true, time does fly by when you're having fun. While I was very happy working for myself, (business had picked up) and doing all my personal development, the time had come to focus on "having a life." I needed to find a healthy outlet for myself and my newfound energy levels. A sport or hobby where I could meet like-minded others and have "wholesome fun" that didn't involve alcohol, bad food or toxic people!

In 2010, I was talking to a customer one day who told me he was a member of a local cycling club that welcomed women. It sounded perfect for me as I had always loved my bike. As a kid I used to cycle to school and back. He kindly gave me the details and in no time at all, I was their newest member. I was really looking forward to being in a sports club. I had never been a member of any type of club. I was a little anxious about meeting new people and was worried that I wouldn't "fit in." However, those nerves didn't stop me. I needed other people in my life and was prepared to push myself out of my comfort zone.

Excitedly, I went shopping for a brand-new road bike. Even though my budget was minimal, I was delighted with my shiny new purchase. Coincidentally it was the exact same blue as my very first bike. I was ready for action on two wheels

"I don't ride a bike to add days to my life, I ride a bike to add life to my days!"

-Unknown

Chapter 8
Life behind handlebars
Dublin 2010

I am so grateful that at a young age my parents taught me how to ride a bike. It was my first lesson in how to be a "big girl." In our house we were raised to be independent and to make things happen. There was no time to slouch, the farm was busy and there was always something to be done. I loved that our family motto was "get up and get on with it" which became the principal life lesson that I took on with mighty gusto. While at different times in my life I took it to the extreme, I wouldn't change a thing. It has made me who I am. I would rather be a hardy "go getter" than a snowflake.

I bet my parents never thought, all those years ago, as they encouraged me to keep pedalling as I wobbled around on my bike that their little girl would grow up to be a world adventurer and cycle some of the most challenging climbs that this earth has to offer.

Fancy balance bikes were not invented back in the 1970s and in our house, there was no need for stabilizers. Instead, Mam or Dad would hold onto the back of my saddle while shouting at me to pedal faster as I furiously tried to coordinate my legs and steer. They gave me and my bike little pushes and stayed close by at first.

Along the side of the curb, we would go, my feet were constantly tempted to touch the floor. It was hard and required a lot of practice.

I learnt on an old blue bike which had no brakes, or so I thought at first. It turned out you had to pedal backwards to make it stop. It had also lost its plastic pedals from overuse; my feet instead were on the metal bars where the pedals were supposed to be. Being the youngest child everything I got was a hand-me-down, a little battered and worn. I was a lot smaller than my two siblings too. While Dad lowered the saddle as far as it would go, the bike was still too big for me initially. I just had to suck it up and manage as best as I could. In time I grew a few inches, and the bike was a perfect fit. To celebrate, he made me wooden blocks to replace the missing pedals and secured them with industrial tape. I was over the moon with my new, top of the range, custom pedals and was not one bit embarrassed by how my bike looked. In the 1970's that's how life was.

The first time I managed to get a little balance my legs were moving rapidly in circles. While the handlebars were shaking, I was moving forward, not exactly in a straight line, but that would come with time. I thought Dad was still holding onto the back of my bike, and I felt safe and happy until I saw him standing over by the garage door. I lost my nerve in an instant and my feet swiftly touched back down to earth. Eagerly I tried again and again. Even on the days when I bashed the shins off myself, fell off and got frustrated, I kept going.

I wanted to be the same as my older siblings who could ride their bikes with ease. They would glide past me on their big bikes as I struggled furiously to get going. Our cousins lived just down the field from our farm, and they could all cycle with ease too. They rode their bikes up to our house and then much to my annoyance I watched as the older boys cycled together down the road to pitch and putt. They were so grown up in my eyes and had so much freedom. There was I, the little sister hopelessly falling off my bike and wobbling around our driveway. I simply had to learn to ride my bike so that I could be part of the gang. Most of all, I wanted my parents to see me improve, be a big, brave girl, and show them that whatever the other kids could do, I could do too.

Eventually, my frustration, tears and bruises turned to confidence and perfect bike riding. Just like my siblings and cousins, I was gliding around the driveway too and joining in all the fun. While my parents may have been pushing me to learn how to ride a bike, the real lessons they taught me were resilience, determination and courage. They also instilled in me the freedom to be my own independent person. Unbeknownst to me at that time, they had given me lifelong tools that would stand to me in future endeavours.

Time passed by and I grew up. As a teenager, I loved cycling up and down to cricket practice. I was rubbish at batting and even worse at bowling thanks to being an awkward left-hander. Apparently being left-handed caused problems for the coaches trying to teach me as well as the bowler who was confused because I was standing the "wrong" way around. I often left cricket practice feeling like I had a disability and wondering why I had bothered to turn up. It was the same when I tried to knit and crochet in school. My yarn was constantly in a tangle, and I lost so many stitches that my "scarf" looked more like Edam cheese. It seemed to me that no one had the patience for me and my "southpaw," so I just gave up.

What I loved about cycling was that it was neither left nor right-handed. I could do it and be the same as everyone else while going places. I adored the feeling of self-reliance and strength it gave me too. I felt like I could do anything when I was on my bike. Somehow, when I was cycling I got superpowers! Even though our farm was uphill, it never occurred to me that it was steep or difficult to reach. I just powered on and pushed my pedals that bit harder when the going got tough until I eventually got home. Nothing was too hard for me when I was on my bike. I had some sort of weird acceptance of effort that came naturally to me. I never complained when I was cycling. Why would I? Cycling was my liberation. It gave me my first taste of travelling solo too, even if it was just going to school or the shops.

As I grew into an adult I continued to cycle whenever possible, even if it was just to the shops or a commute to work. While I couldn't cycle when I worked on the ship I enjoyed working out on the stationary bike in the gym. It was wonderful to pedal hard for an hour while looking out at the ocean and the endless blue skies.

When I sat on my brand-new road bike and headed off for my first day in the cycling club I felt like a kid again. All the old feelings of freedom and strength came flooding back to me. I was ready to conquer Dublin on my bike. I need not have been anxious about being the "newbie." I was welcomed with open arms. The cycling group that I started with met every Saturday. It was for ladies only and I liked that. I didn't know any other sporty girls and I was glad to make some female acquaintances. They were extremely fit and friendly, as well as very nice towards me. I enjoyed the little sisterhood that I became a part of.

On my very first day I was told that we were going to cycle a whopping fifty kilometres along the coast and go to some posh coffee shop for cake. The group was very specific about the pit stop; it was non-negotiable as most of the women fancied the twins that owned it!

I didn't care about the men; I was worried sick that I wouldn't manage that sort of distance. Funnily enough, I hadn't been able to cycle during my time on the ship. I was apprehensive about my lung capacity too from all my years of being a good-time girl. While I had been to hundreds of spinning classes over the years and even had a certificate to teach it, being on a moving bike, in a group (peloton), with traffic was nerve-wracking, to say the least.

Our little posse rolled out and our very kind leader shouted instructions at us. I didn't understand what they were for but in time I learnt that they were to protect the group from potholes and other hazards. I loved that we were working as a team and looked out for each other. As much as I enjoyed working solo, it was wonderful on weekends not to have to do everything for myself, by myself. While I loved riding my bike, I enjoyed the company and chats more.

As I was new to road cycling and on a budget, I didn't want to spend more money on "bike stuff." However, when I joined the club I was a little embarrassed that I was cycling in my runners and best gym clothes. They were all I had in my wardrobe but thankfully my "bike sisters" were very helpful and gave me lots of helpful advice. They were "clipped into" their pedals by special shoes. They make you faster, but I was a little concerned about my clumsiness and felt that those pedals could wait until I was more experienced in the traffic. They also looked so classy and lovely too, like professional cyclists in their very fancy clothes. They even had pockets on the back of their jerseys to hold their bananas and keys. Not like me, I was wearing a "bum-bag!" To top off their "must have" items, they wore cycling shorts with big cushion inserts. I thought it made them look like they had a baboon's backside, but I was very quick to realise just why they were wearing monkey shorts. I invested in a pair of those shorts the very next day!

Every Saturday enthusiastically I jumped out of bed and couldn't wait to meet the girls: our spin had quickly become the highlight of my week. Slowly but surely each month I bought a new item of clothing or equipment until eventually, I looked the part too. As well as fitting in style-wise, I started to make lots of new friends who shared the same passion for the outdoors as me. I was even added to our group's corresponding email list which made me feel all warm and fuzzy inside. I had been accepted. I was finally part of a gang, a real one, and had found my tribe.

Each club spin improved my cycling prowess as well as my familiarity with every coffee shop in Ireland. It didn't matter to us how far the café was from home, the goal of the weekend was to get there, eat cake and come home. Having others to explore the countryside and ride with helped me to push my social boundaries while challenging my physical and mental endurance every single week. After a few months, our group accepted some men to join our Saturday spins. I was dreading it; I was worried that the men would think I was a lunatic or one of those "crazy women" I had often heard men talking about. While they didn't know my past I just didn't want to feel under pressure to behave a certain way around them. I liked my "girl power" Saturdays, I was in my comfort zone and really didn't want it to change. However, life had different plans and I had to welcome them, the same way as I had been welcomed into the fold.

Admittedly, chatting to the men in our group was a little easier than I expected as we rode shoulder to shoulder, and I never had to look them directly in the eye! Plus we were moving, there was momentum and other moving parts in the equation. Also, our conversations were light-hearted, we talked rubbish when cycling! Nobody cared about my past, what I worked at or my social standing and vice versa. It turned out I didn't have to impress anyone or "beat off competition" to get the man as they were all married. It was relaxed and light-hearted. We, all genders, were there to cycle, have a good time, get out of the house and eat cake. It also happened by chance, that when we got punctures or mechanical problems, the men loved to take over, get dirty and show off to the ladies. Personally, I was happy to let them knock themselves out, sure I could do it, but I didn't want to get oil on my new kit!

No longer a smoker, it wasn't long before I got much fitter. My body recovered surprisingly well from all the damage I had done to it. I looked even better than I had after my trip to India. I was toned, fit and glowing from all my exercise and being outdoors. Even though I was eating a lot of cake, it didn't show on my belly or affect my mood as I was creating so many "feel good" hormones on my bike. Would you believe it, I was not even afraid to look in the mirror anymore, in fact, I quite liked what I saw. Cycling may have changed my physique, but more importantly, it helped to change my mental state regarding my body image for the better.

My physical endurance and resilience improved no end as the distances we rode continuously increased. We started going much further afield, I couldn't believe it when I cycled my very first 100 kilometres'. I was shattered for days after it, but I was so proud of myself. I was over my apprenticeship and was a bona fide cycling club member. I started going on cycling weekends away in other parts of Ireland to take part in events which had thousands of other cyclists on the route. They were a big deal, because I never imagined when I joined the club that it would include travelling and being invited to places with others. It was a lot more than I had bargained for and I was ecstatic. I had never travelled around Ireland, in fact, I'm ashamed to say it, but I never opened that chapter in my atlas. I didn't know half of the places we went to existed and I was shocked at how beautiful Ireland was. When I worked on the cruise ship, passengers used to bore me stupid with tales of their trips to Ireland. They kept going on about how green and picturesque it was. I never listened to them, I nodded my head and smiled like a fool but in my head, I was off on the horizon looking for our next exotic destination. Yet when I started to cycle around my homeland, I understood what they loved and remembered about their visit. I too became enthusiastic about our little island. It was like a hidden treasure to me that was begging to be discovered. I started to spend time researching, reading and planning trips to all the beautiful places that were on my own "turf!"

It didn't take long for me to upgrade my bike either, 8 months in fact. While I loved my blue road bike it was actually too big for me and rather poor quality. (I was also ripped off by the guy I bought it from.) I replaced it with a gorgeous red and white Orbea road bike which I loved like it was my best friend. (I actually used to talk to it and tell it how great it was!) Together we clocked up thousands of kilometres and burnt just as many calories from delicious cakes. I was happiest when I was whizzing around on my Orbea while feeling the wind brush off my face, surrounded by nature and the elements. As soon as I sat on the saddle I instantly forgot about work, problems, life, or anything else that was on my mind. I was doing what I loved and nothing else mattered to me. It was my own form of therapy, meditation and happy pill all rolled into one.

Luckily for me, both my travel addiction and love of cycling were very compatible. When I gave myself time, I found freedom, headspace and my tribe. From the comfort of my saddle, I have explored the world, cycled to dizzying heights, gone on outlandish adventures and found out what I am truly made of.

Chapter 9
Death Road
Bolivia 2010

My first mega solo adventure was in 2010. Five years had passed since my "episode." While I was living my best life I had itchy feet. An extended holiday, indeed, a trip of a lifetime was required.

My plan was to escape the winter darkness by going to the southern hemisphere to enjoy their summer. Sydney, Australia was my chosen destination. I couldn't wait to spend New Year's Eve on the harbour and enjoy the magnificent firework display over the Opera House. However, instead of flying there directly, I chose to go via South America, as you do! It seemed like a perfectly logical thing to do, besides, the price for a round-the-world ticket was actually cheaper than a return flight to Oz. So in order to be cost-efficient, I bought it and blocked off five weeks in my diary.

As you know I had been doing a lot of personal development over the years, but I never ever expected to have an epiphany on my first flight. When I settled into my fourteen-hour flight from Amsterdam to Lima, the capital of Peru, I had some sort of mad, accidental "Aha" moment. As soon as the airplane door closed, out of nowhere a great big sigh of relief left my body, it felt like it had come up from my toes. I was so surprised I looked around to see who made the noise. However, judging from my neighbour's astonished expression, I was suddenly aware that it had been me who made the weird sound!

It was a tremendous release of stress and anxiety that left my body. Even though I was doing great in life, I must have been carrying something deeper around in the pit of my soul for years. It had finally found the right time and place to leave me, as if through some sort of escape hatch. I felt lighter, my body had purged, and I was instantly cleansed. I think subconsciously, I was making mental space for all the adventures, and new experiences that were waiting for me on my world expedition. Was I excited? You bet I was.

Strapped into my seat as the plane hurtled down the runway and we took off for a new continent I had everything I needed at that moment. It was just me, myself and I, and it felt perfect. I was headed out into the unknown once again. Just like when I boarded the cruise ship, no one knew me in South America, and I was free to think and feel any way I wanted to. I could do whatever the heck I liked, there was no one else to answer to or consider as my backpack and I headed out into uncharted territory. I absolutely loved feeling so carefree.

While I had changed a lot of things in my life during the previous few years, I felt the time had come for me to be even more courageous. I was brave on my bike, but I needed to throw off the shackles, dig a lot deeper around my mental state and ditch limiting beliefs that still wandered into my head at times.

In the peace and quiet of the aircraft cabin, along with the gentle hum of the engines, I could clearly hear myself think. It was as if the depth of my soul was suddenly awake, it was a whole new feeling of aliveness. My deepest sense of self, (sorry if it sounds corny) had come to the surface to introduce herself to the world. Many thoughts rushed around in my head, some were good, others were bad and just for good measure some were incredibly horrible. My brain was frantically reshuffling my internal filing cabinet so that it could shred the paperwork that no longer served me. Even though my head was being bombarded from all angles, I knew I was OK.

I was in a safe space and had the courage to sit with myself while the reconstruction happened. They were just thoughts after all; I didn't have to pay them any attention. They were like dark clouds trying to cover a blue sky and thankfully, I was able to let them float on by without causing a storm. I was sure it was a test! It was as if I was being challenged, provoked almost to see if I would fall back into my old ways or if I was ready to move up a level in the game of life.

I was very aware that a lot of the thoughts that were surfacing weren't really mine at all. On reflection, they were mostly pre-conditioned by society, my demographics as well as my nearest and dearest. When I observed those thoughts, I recognised that they were in fact not mine, most went against my values and beliefs. I needed to stop carrying them. I was done with other people's expectations and opinions of me.

Sitting alone on the plane seat with headphones on, I took out a pen and paper and began writing furiously. All my thoughts, feelings, deepest hurts, sadness as well as hopes and dreams spilt onto the page. I basically vomited up all my repressed feelings and purged until there was nothing left inside me. It was the perfect time and place for it to happen, there was nowhere to run or hide on the plane! I could have popped on a movie to distract myself, but I wasn't going to miss the opportunity that had presented itself to me. Besides I had done so much poking around in my head over the years that it was not exactly new to me. I was a brave woman who was taking responsibility and action to live a purposeful and fulfilling life through travel and experiences. My eyes were opened even wider to endless possibilities, there was no going backwards.

Landing on a new continent I incredibly felt lucky to have three and a half weeks there to travel through Peru, Bolivia and Chile. I also had all the time in the world to think about what had surfaced for me during my flight.

It wasn't all intense, deep thinking on my trip! Far from it in fact. I was there to have the time of my life while seeing a new part of the world. Bolivia is still one of the top-ranking countries that I have ever been to, in fact, it is consistently in my top three. It was like stepping into an old Wild West movie and I enjoyed every single minute of it. Right up my street, it was rough and ready, dusty with volcanoes, thermal springs, deserts and massive cacti. I witnessed thousands of pink flamingos going about their business. They were perched in lakes that were red from the algae and microorganisms living in them. Bolivia was out of this world. If you told me I was on Mars I would have believed you. Bolivia exceeded all my expectations and truly fascinated me. There was so much to explore, see and do.

I arrived at the salt flats of the Salar de Uyuni via an exhilarating 4 x 4 jeep safari. We drove through the deserts for hours which gave me the opportunity to gaze at spectacular scenery while feeling deeply happy and rejuvenated. I relaxed and sat with my thoughts while watching a beautiful sunset at the shore of Lake Titicaca. I also spent hours on long bus journeys, so while I was looking out of the window and watching the world go by, I had ample time to reflect on how I wanted my life story to go from that moment onwards.

From the moment I arrived at La Paz airport, (the highest capital in the world at 3,630 metres), I was smitten. I had taken a very short flight from Cuzco in Peru to get there. Stepping off the plane I didn't have far to walk from the aircraft to the terminal. The thin air at such a high altitude hit me hard. Gasping to catch my breath I practically crawled on my hands and knees into the building and wondered if I had suddenly developed asthma or if one of my lungs had collapsed.

My health concerns were soon dismissed though when the passport official tried to get a bribe from me as I entered the country. There was a tiny tear in my passport on one of the insignificant pages that no one cares about. He kept pointing to the damage and shouting at me in his gravelly Bolivian accent. Unaware of what he was getting at, I stood there smiling at him through the Perspex screen like a complete idiot. I was so thrilled to be in another new country, Bolivia of all places, whoever would have thought that little old me would be there? The unkempt passport official with too many buttons undone on his scruffy shirt continued to shout at me. His

Spanish words were coming out of his mouth at tremendous speed, it was all gibberish to me, I had no clue what he was saying. While the other border control officers were working through their line of passengers, mine was holding up the queue and was still blabbing frantically at me!

My Spanish back then was zero and, honestly, it never occurred to me that a passport official might try to extort a bribe from me in the arrivals hall. However, after spending time in Bolivia nothing would surprise me. He finally cracked under the pressure of talking to a grinning fool. He was getting nothing out of me other than a big happy, smiley head. His face had turned bright red, sweat was pouring off his forehead and his voice was wobbling. Exasperated and annoyed that the little lady who was travelling alone didn't panic and pay him a "gratuity" he finally quit. He grabbed his stamper, permitted me entry and duly flung my passport back at me. It was only later in my hostel when I told the receptionist what had happened he calmly told me that the official was looking for a cash bribe. Imagine that?

That was my welcome to Bolivia, a country that would be hard to forget for its sights, altitude and corruption. While I did not have long there I definitely had time for a cycling adventure. I had read so much about a one-day cycling trip from La Paz, along a road known as the DEATH ROAD! (El Camino de la Muerte).

There was absolutely no way I was going to miss that excursion. Once upon a time, it was a main road, which is horrifying to think about when you see it. The road was high up in the Andes and ran along the edge of the cliffs.

Four other tourists and I departed La Paz in a minivan with our guides, along with a trailer full of mountain bikes and kit behind us. It was great getting to know the other tourists, we were full of chat, excitement and anticipation. When you travel solo you always meet lovely people and on an excursion like that, they were always going to be like-minded (and "cool!")

From the city, we drove even higher for two hours until we eventually arrived at a little car park at a height of 4,700 metres above sea level in the Andes. At that altitude, the air was even thinner than at the airport. It was also much cooler, and I could feel the UV rays searing into my skin given we were so close to the sun. Yet, I was in my element and could not stop smiling as we prepared the bikes and put on our oversized, smelly, shabby boiler suits.

Death Road was a rough trail rather than a "proper" road: there were sheer drops on one side of the road down into gullies as deep as the Grand Canyon. There were tiny, almost useless safety barriers on the edge of the road which added to the danger. There were some limited spaces for vehicles to pass each other, but I would not have liked to have been the vehicle on the outside, hanging over the edge, staring in the face of death. When I travelled along the route I couldn't believe that it had once been a functioning main thoroughfare.

(The road was originally constructed to connect the capital city, La Paz, to the Amazon back in the 1930s and was called the North Yungas Road. However, it soon became known as Death Road due to so many people losing their life in accidents. Eventually, (thankfully) the road was closed to traffic when a new, safer main road was completed in 2006.)

As a constant reminder of the many tragedies, little stone crosses appeared every so often along the side of the road, each one signifying a final resting place. When I looked down over the cliff edge, way down in the foliage, I could see, tangled in the vegetation, cars, trucks and vans that met their fate over the years. It was terribly upsetting knowing there were so many victims involved in the accidents, and I especially did not want to think about how awful their deaths were. Even though Death Road was officially closed to traffic, the route was the most perfect adventure cycling track in the world, and I had to complete it.

Death road was eighty kilometres of gravelly grit with great big dirty puddles to splash through. My mountain bike was in good condition. I doubly checked the brakes before departure and was confident that they were working well. I didn't care that it was the most uncomfortable saddle in the world as long as the bike was safe, that was all that mattered. The road only took a few hours to complete, plus there were plenty of photo stops throughout the cycle which gave me a little comfort break as well as quality time to admire the giant Andes.

Twisting and turning, we cycled along the road with earth's natural wall on one side and a bottomless pit of vegetation on the other. It was a jungle down there, lush, dense and green with all sorts of weird and wonderful shaped leaves poking up to say hello. The air was so fresh and even though it was humid as hell up there, thankfully there were sporadic waterfalls cascading down the valley and raining over us, which was enough to cool me down.

It was exhilarating, fun and wonderfully crazy all at the same, freewheeling downhill and splashing along the dirt road. My helmet kept clattering the side of my head whenever I went over big bumps. Simultaneously, every time I ploughed over a large rock I was lifted up off the saddle, high into the air while trying to hang on for dear life. I was bouncing along, screaming and laughing at the same time as I went in and out of holes. I was high on life on nature's rollercoaster.

Our little "posse" was genuinely fun too. We were buzzing, whooping and hollering as we rode along the route. Exhausted and elated, we finished our cycle down Death Road covered in dust and dirt. We "high fived" each other's hands and huddled in for a group photo. We enjoyed every moment of our bike ride and most importantly, we arrived alive.

There was a small town at the end of the route called Yolosa, all the way down at 1,500 meters above sea level. Our spectacularly scenic cycle had taken us a massive 3600 meters downhill through the Andes Mountain range. While we relaxed at the finish line with a well-earned beer we were bubbly and full of chat. Excitedly we exchanged stories about our travels and adventures in South America, and each had something to contribute to the conversation. That's what I loved most about backpacking. Not only were we all on the same beaten track, more or less, but we also had the same mentality too. I was thrilled to be assured that there were so many other people like me out there. Travelling solo opened up so many possibilities, new friends and unfamiliar places to me. As I said before, the best part of going it alone was I had nothing to hide or prove to anyone; no one had any opinion or prejudgement of me, and it was liberating.

Loaded up and ready to go for the second part of the day trip, we were driven to the small town of Coroico. We arrived at a beautiful hotel with a terrace which overlooked the entire valley. The vista was spectacular. I was impressed by the sheer scale of the mountains when I was cycling through them but when I was there in the hotel, I could relax and really take in the grand scale of the area. There was a deep, dense forest as far as I could see. Sporadically misty clouds and mini rainbows formed where waterfalls were spraying water droplets into the air. I wish I could describe the sheer depth and scale of the landscape, the enormity of the mountains and the noises from exotic birds. At best, all I can say, it was like a scene from a Jurassic Park movie. Sometimes, unexpectedly, the leaves rustled quite dramatically, and I really hoped it was just the wind.

We had full use of the hotel, including showers and the pool, for a few hours to relax and enjoy. It was a beautiful boutique hacienda painted in a welcoming creamy lemon with dusky terracotta roof tiles. The doors and windows were each flung wide open allowing the breeze to gently waft through the large reception area. Sunbeams shone brightly through the large banquet room where our delicious lunch was served.

The hotel gardens were strikingly beautiful with bright pink flowers trailing up the walls adding contrast to the lemon paint. It was really luxurious; surprisingly so given the price we had paid for the day trip. However we were not complaining, it was relaxing and exactly what we needed after our busy morning.

Dipping in the pool, the water was so soothing to my achy sore muscles and bones that felt like they had been rattled around in a bag. After my paddle, I crawled onto one of the comfortable sun loungers in the sun and had a snooze in the sun. It had been the most perfect day.

Our guides had given us a departure time and like all considerate tourists, we went back to the van on time. However, the guides and the driver, all three of them, were passed out across the back seats in the van. Drunk as lords. Paralytic in fact. We had only left them for a few hours, and they were ossified! It was like a scene from a movie, they lay there, limp, only for their snoring and dribbling I could have sworn they were dead. They reeked of cheap alcohol and body odour; we couldn't get in the van because the smell would have killed us!

The five of us were astonished but thankfully we all agreed in a split second, there was no chance we were going with them. How could we? It was almost three hours to drive back to the city, through the valleys, uphill on twisty dangerous roads and it was going to be dark.

In their drunken haze, our guides heard the commotion. Mumbling and slurring something they started to stir. One by one they woke up and realised that they were in big trouble. The guests were holding a mutiny. Springing into instant sobriety which I am still amazed at, from ossified to level-headed in 60 seconds, they desperately tried to convince us to get in the van with them. They pleaded with us that they would lose their jobs if they arrived back in La Paz without their guests. Unfortunately for them, our decision was set in stone. We were not, under circumstances, travelling back with them.

Thank goodness the hotel came to our rescue. They kindly helped our little motley crew of stranded tourists to arrange a taxi back to the city. We didn't care how much it was going to cost us, we just wanted to get back alive!

Our unlikely taxi driving hero turned up in a jalopy of a car. Fortunately for us, he was completely sober and genuinely nice too. I think he may have put on his best shirt for us. Even though it was missing a few buttons and gaped a bit from his protruding belly he was clean and doing his best to present himself well. Giving us a great big smile which showed off his buckled teeth that were covered in yellow tobacco stains, he was our very own superhero. Patiently we waited while he exchanged pleasantries with the hotel staff - he was thanking them profusely for getting him the fare of a lifetime.

He was over the top thrilled with his VIP guests. He was acting like a chauffeur that was working for royalty as he held open the door and motioned for us to pile in. While the car was old and rattling, it was roadworthy. There were even enough seats for us all, as it was some sort of station wagon with three rows of seats. The Argentinian chap took the passenger seat up front. He was our designated co-pilot whose job was to keep "Mr Hero Driver" company and awake for the trip.

The car was well worn to say the least, but we didn't care. Bolivia was a poor country so we couldn't be fussy, plus the choice was to go with a drunk driver or go in an old car. All aboard our chariot, we were sitting comfortably and ready for departure. Next stop La Paz. We proceeded into the long journey which took us back up the valley to the city via winding roads, through the depths of jungles, high up in the Andes.

Darkness was coming swiftly; it had been a very full and long day. It was unbelievable and I don't understand why, but in Bolivia, they drove their vehicles with their lights OFF! They only turned them on when they saw another car coming towards them. Bonkers! Surely that defeated the entire purpose of having lights on the car. But, as much as I would have liked to try, who was I to change an entire nation's driving logic?

After three long hours of twisting roads we arrived back in the city of La Paz. Coming through the dark mountain roads, we were welcomed by the city lights which were starting to prepare for the evening's festivities. The main thoroughfare through the city was the best place for us to be dropped off. It was a great big ugly dual carriageway, which quite obnoxiously split the city in two. They say New York never sleeps but South America was always on the go too, everyone was busy and up to something. There was an enthusiastic sense of hustle and bustle on the entire continent, it was like a beehive on steroids. There was so much life and productivity in every major South American city I have ever been to. They also know how to party. Music was very much a part of being in South America. Everywhere I went, no matter what time, day or night, there was music blaring from some window somewhere, being drowned out by the sound of numerous loud and happy voices with plenty of clinking glasses.

We were so glad to be back in the city and in one piece. We thanked our hero driver profusely as we paid him. He was smiling from ear to ear, shaking our hands and saluting us. Job done; he was clutching his hard-earned wad of money as he pulled away. We all knew he had overcharged us, but it hardly mattered, he absolutely deserved every peso we gave him.

We agreed to go to the tour company office together the next day. We needed strength in numbers, and I needed a translator! We wanted our photos that the guides had taken of the day trip.

We all were crazy with curiosity too, we wanted to know what happened to the guides when they returned to the office with no guests. Can you imagine taking five tourists out for the day and coming home with none? If you lost one you might be forgiven, two at best. But all five, well that was just careless. We had a good laugh about the day over a post-trauma beer. We all admitted that we were relieved to have had each other throughout the adventure for support. In the bar, Diego the Argentinian, who had been sitting up front with the driver, admitted to us that there were no brakes on our rescue taxi. Our superhero had been using the hand brake to slow the car down on corners. Poor Diego had been at his wits' end and was terrified for the entire journey back. We had travelled through the Andes, in the dark, with no lights on, for three hours in that car. On the plus side, our driver was sober, and it had only cost €30 between the five of us! I loved Bolivia for its "crazy" ways.

As for the guides, well we never heard what happened to them. When we went to the office en masse, the manager flippantly threw a photo disk (it was 2010) and a t-shirt at each of us. He never looked us in the eye or said a word. He just shook his head and seemed to be annoyed with us. Perhaps he was shell-shocked or maybe he was just relieved that we had not been kidnapped. God only knows what story the guides had spun him; after all nothing was unbelievable in Bolivia.

From Bolivia, my amazing trip continued onwards to Chile which was wonderful. I had a stopover in Auckland, New Zealand which I knew well from my cruise ship days.

I spent a week in Fiji where I enjoyed Christmas day on the beach while snorkelling and relaxing in the sun. From there I flew to my final destination in Sydney, Australia. I was mesmerized as I watched the most incredible firework display I had ever seen. As I welcomed in another new year I was overcome with joy and excitement for whatever 2011 had in store for me.

It was a trip of a lifetime in more ways than one. My whirl-wind five-week circumnavigation of the world brought me to many wonderful places but most importantly, it gave me valuable time and space to come face to face with a deeper knowledge and acceptance of myself. I loved being on my own on that trip. It was the first time I one hundred percent looked out for myself and started to become my own best friend. I loved being free to come and go as I pleased while creating wonderful memories for myself. It was on the trip too that I became addicted to taking photographs of anything and everything that would forever remind me of my adventures.

Flying home from Australia to Ireland was long but I enjoyed every minute of it. I took time to reminisce and to reflect on my wonderful trip. Taking out my pen and journal I let my imagination run riot and made a bucket list of the endless places and crazy adventures I want to see and do before my time is up on this earth. Nothing was out of bounds, even a trip to the moon made the list. Sure you have to think and dream big. Little did I know as I made my way home, that trip around the world and my bucket list would spur me on for the rest of my life to see and do more than I ever thought possible.

Death Road

Chapter 10
Tortoise tactics
France 2014

After my trip round the world my piggy bank was put on red alert for massive savings and every single cent that I could spare went into it. Thankfully as I was never into fashion or expensive handbags and as I was no longer a smoker, I was able to save up enough each year to have an "annual trip of a lifetime!"

One day I came across a wonderful set of rules to live by which was created by the Dalai Lama. He advised "once a year, go somewhere you have never been before." Who was I to argue with a spiritual leader? I took that quote and pinned it to my mirror as a daily reminder that travel was an investment in myself.

I also attached my new bucket list to the inside of my wardrobe along with cuttings from travel brochures and magazines. I made a colourful collage of landmarks, mountain ranges, beaches and animals that I wanted to see up close. Every day while I was getting dressed I stared at my pictures and fantasised about my next destination. While my vision board was my constant source of inspiration to work harder, save more and travel further, it also gave me valuable headspace. As long as I was daydreaming about my travel goals I wasn't worried or stressed about anything.

In 2011 I returned to India and spent a month over Christmas in Goa. It was a very different visit from my previous one. There was no ashram for a start, instead I stayed in a lovely little guest house which was cheap as chips as I rented it for a "long term let." I relaxed for a few hours every day while sunbathing on the most splendid beaches Goa had to offer in glorious sunshine. While I did go to a Yoga class every morning, it was just not at the crack of dawn. After my classes I swam in the tranquil waters of the turquoise blue Indian Ocean. After my busy day, every evening at sunset I joined in with the "hippy" party on the beach which celebrated the end of the day with a bonfire, drums and dancing. I loved the freedom of expression that Goa brought out in people. Some were throwbacks from the 1960's who had never left. To be honest, I think they had the right idea. They never got caught up in the madness of the rat race or conformity. Sure, there were any number of drugs there if you wanted to enhance the experience, but I wasn't interested in that, I didn't need them. I was more than happy enough to let my inner hippy bubble back up to the surface and dance freely while "sober."

I ate copious amounts of rice and tonnes of fresh fruit too. My four weeks in Goa were like a health farm with lots of chill-out time to read trashy novels and sleep in the sun. Most importantly though, I made some time for another self-appraisal. Since my round the world trip I had made it my business to have regular "mini life check-ups" with myself but at the end of the year, I had a formal and in-depth review with my mental health, feelings, goals and bucket list! I liked to analyse my progress and make necessary amendments for maximum success. My biggest and most telling question to myself was, "am I happy in my life and do I like myself?"

I loved sitting on a sun lounger contemplating my answers. It was especially beneficial and meaningful to me to write down, brainstorm and mind map my revelations. I gained clarity from my visual tools. I even allowed my creative and artistic side to shine by using different coloured pens and doodling in my journal! While that might sound childish or even like a multinational boardroom meeting, it's what worked for me. I was always a very organised person and when I was in school I thought that pie charts and graphs were the best thing since sliced bread! By the end of my trip, my journal looked like a mash up between a comic and a PowerPoint presentation. It didn't matter to me how it looked, I had achieved my objective and had a new three-year plan and progress targets in place. There were even bonuses built into my "contract" too, naturally they were in the form of more exotic trips.

In 2013 my trip of a lifetime was a bit bonkers! I went to the Arctic Circle on a snowmobile safari for my 40th birthday. While it was minus 35 degrees my most memorable moment of that trip was lying flat on my back in the snow while looking up at the northern lights as they danced through the heavens. They were just as beautiful as I had imagined. Pale green, wispy hues floated and swirled in the dark sky moving to their very own romantic rhythm. On another occasion I lay once again on my back in the snow under the jet-black sky. Being so remote and far from civilization had its advantages. I could see just about every star in the galaxy shining brightly, they were sparkling like diamonds that appeared to twinkle through the darkness. I was captivated by the splendid show the entire universe was putting on for me as countless shooting stars pinged across the vast panorama in all directions. They looked like mini fireworks rocketing across the heavens trying to meet each other. When I was in the Andes I felt small and a little insignificant in the grand scheme of things, however while I was in the Arctic, I felt really humbled to be connected to the endless universe. In some way, I felt like my ancestors were giving me a sneak peek into heaven and eternity.

In contrast, there was a wild skiing trip in Austria where I discovered the world of après-ski and joined in wholeheartedly. Like everything I have done in my life I did that to the best of my ability too. Even though I was more mature in years I was in my element dancing on tables and doing shots after a long day on two skis. It was the perfect holiday to let my hair down, have fun and go a bit (a lot) mad.

To continue the celebration of turning 40 years old, I ran a half marathon in France around the vineyards. That might sound like nothing special except it was also to celebrate the release of that year's Beaujolais Nouveau (red wine.) It was obligatory to drink wine while running the route. Just to make sure I didn't spill any I stopped and guzzled. I was part of a women's running group at that time and the entire congregation went on the trip. There were 35 middle aged Irish women all dressed in completely over the top Irish paraphernalia (we looked like leprechauns on acid) running riot in the province of Beaujolais. As we ran through the stunning countryside we drank copious amounts of red wine and ate French cheese with crackers. It was very civilized in all honesty, and our numerous refreshments stops certainly took the effort out of the actual run. Needless to say, running on a full tummy while a little drunk was a novelty and not something I would normally condone but you only live once so what the heck!

I had a wonderful year, full of mini celebrations. I had entered into a whole new decade in my life, I was older and wiser, dare I say it, and I felt incredible in myself. It did cross my mind though, since I was forty, that perhaps I should start to think about "settling down." Thankfully that thought only lasted a nano second and then I broke into rapturous laughter when I realised what I had "said." There was no chance I was settling down unless it was into a seat for a long-haul flight.

In 2014 I was lucky enough to take another solo trip to South America where I had the good sense to only explore one country, Ecuador. Once again I thoroughly enjoyed being in South America and spent all of my time outdoors. I went on an exhilarating white water rafting trip through raging rapids. I went hiking up an extinct volcano to high altitude and sailed around the Galapagos islands. My favourite place that I visited on that trip was a nature sanctuary where I got to meet and fall in love with the giant tortoises. I thought they had lovely, friendly little smiles on their wrinkly faces. They each looked like a wise and kind old person. I loved their slow, gentle demeanour and while they had a hard shell on the outside, I just knew that there was a big, mushy softness to them on the inside.

I met a lifelong friend on that trip too. I was out for a run and stopped at a viewpoint overlooking the town of Baños. Rachel from New Zealand was there enjoying the vista too with her top-notch camera that I would learn in time was her trademark. We struck up a conversation about photography and travel which was an obvious ice breaker.

After just a few minutes chatting it was obvious that we were very alike in many ways. Like me, she was also travelling alone and was single too. We also seemed to have identical itineraries which was a little spooky. On that particular day when we met, we were both on the same trail and were headed for another viewpoint higher in the valley. Without any hesitation we joined forces for the journey. As we hiked up the side of the mountain we chatted end-lessly about anything and everything. Myself and Rachel were like peas in a pod. Our views and outlook on life were similar too even though we lived on opposite sides of the world. It was refreshing to talk to someone who I could discuss global politics and current affairs with, as well as men and dating disasters! We became instant friends that day. We were both staying in the same town for a few nights and met up for dinners and drinks too. Even though neither Ireland nor New Zealand had qualified for the world cup in Brazil in 2014, we shouted loudly at the TV as we watched the live matches that were on in the bars.

It was great to have such good company and another fellow female solo traveller to chat with about life. Like us all, Rachel had had her own cross to bear but thankfully she had found her own coping mechanism. We learnt a lot from each other over the few days we shared in Ecuador. You could say that we were meant to meet. While I think that's true, we were also both doing what we loved and were in our happy place. I think, really, we were birds of a feather flocking together. Would you believe, we have kept in touch all through the years and even met up for a night out in London in 2016. Thanks to social media and video calls we continue to this day to have long conversations about absolutely anything and everything.

When I returned home from Ecuador, in the space of less than a week it was time for me to go back to Dublin airport and queue up in departures. I was going to France with some of the gang from my cycling club. We were registered to participate in a huge cycling event called La Marmotte. I was very excited about the trip. It was my first actual "proper" cycling holiday as opposed to a holiday with a bit of cycling.

While I was not really that strong a cyclist in 2014, I was happy with my cycling ability and was enjoying life immensely on two wheels. Even though I was attending many cycling events and covering good mileage I was still cycling in the "chat while moving your legs group." We may not have been the fastest bunch on the road, but we didn't care, we were happy with our speed, weekly achievements and gossip updates.

When the opportunity came to team up with other cyclists from my club for a trip to the French Alps in July 2014 I snatched it with both hands. However, just to be sure that I would manage travelling as part of a group, I made sure that I had a little sneaky safety net for myself. I paid extra to have my own room so that I would always have my little escape hatch to retreat to if I needed time out. Plus, since ultimately we would each have to cycle the route at our own pace, there was a good chance that I would end up riding a lot of the route on my own. I didn't mind that at all, in fact it suited me perfectly. I could still be "Miss Independent Solo Traveller" while being part of the gang for dinners and fun. It was the best of both worlds in one holiday.

Without hesitation I booked my spot and then did my research. It turned out that the Marmotte was an iconic, circular route through the French alps and a whopping 174 kilometres long. There were four tough climbs on the route, which were all very notable from being featured many times on the Tour de France.

The Marmotte route starts off in the quaint town of Bourg d'Oisans at the foot of the Alpe d'Huez, then heads northwest for the first climb, the Col du Glandon, the top of which is 1,924m meters above sea level.

After every climb comes a downhill. There is a super-fast descent into the town of Saint-Colomban-des-Villards. Continuing, the circle turns east to the second summit, the Telegraphe. The lowest peak on the route, it's a mere 1,556 meters above the sea. From the Telegraphe the route turns South through the beautiful, idyllic ski resort of Valloire.

Continuing south, the third and highest climb of the day, the Col du Galibier awaits. A "must-do climb" for all cyclists, it is one of those box ticking, buy the t-shirt achievements. It is the icing on the cake for the day, with its peak at an altitude of 2,646 meters above sea level to be exact. Expect snow up there, even in July.

The route finally turns west to close the circle and bring the riders back through the start line at Bourg d'Oisans. In order to continue the route cyclists must cross the timing mat before the cut-off deadline at 6:15pm, or it's game over.

For those that do make the cut off time there is one last push to the grand finale, the fourth and last climb. The Alpe d'Huez might be just fourteen kilometres long but it's notoriously tough. It consists of 21 switchbacks which zig- zag up to 1,860 metres above sea level to the finish line.

Over the course of the day I was going to gain an elevation over 5,000 metres in elevation. Just for perspective, Mount Everest is 8,849 metres high. So over the day my little bike and I would climb more than halfway up it! Our highest mountain in Ireland is Carrauntoohil in Kerry which is a mere 1,038 metres high. I walked up and down that one afternoon.

While the Marmotte route was going to be a huge challenge for me, even after looking at the route, it never dawned on me that it might be out of my depth. It simply never occurred to me to doubt my ability or think that I might fail. When I looked at the route map all I saw were fabulous locations to cycle through.

Maybe I just have a different outlook on challenges to others. I fully believe that I can accomplish anything I commit to, it might take me all day or ten years more than I thought but I know without any morsel of doubt that I will achieve what I set out to achieve (eventually)!

Sometimes that childish naivety is a blessing. I have signed up for events regardless of whether they are good or bad for me. I have run, walked and crawled through three marathons but I never quit. Even when it is to my own detriment I won't give up. Subsequently I have flogged many a "dead horse" in both relationships and friendships. I never want to give in to failure and will try to see a way through to the bitter end. On the positive side, my "I'm no quitter" mentality has given me the gumption to go on outlandish trips and cycle iconic mountains.

My trip of a lifetime to cycle a portion of the Tour de France started on a hot July day in 2014 when our plane arrived in Lyon, France from Dublin. Piled into a minivan for our transit to the Alps, all fourteen of us in the cycling group were in great spirits. There was so much excitement in our bus, we were full of chatter and hope. We were on our way to the mountains to cycle in the tyre marks of cycling legends. Ireland's own Stephen Roche had tackled those very same climbs on his way to winning the Tour de France in 1987. Now it was our turn to conquer them.

While our little gang were all in the same club, we were a complete mish mash of abilities. There were some extraordinarily strong cyclists who were highly driven by having tonnes of testosterone. Then there were a few slower riders, notably me. The group was very encouraging though, and they were sure that we would all complete the route "no bother." However when I caught my very first glimpse of the mountains, which reached high up into the clouds, suddenly I began to have heart palpitations!

The sheer size and scale of the landscape hit me with a very harsh dose of reality, and it only dawned on me then what I had actually signed up for. When our minibus turned a corner and started to crawl up the infamous Alpe d'Huez I gulped. My heart was pounding loudly, my jaw dropped, and my eyes popped from their sockets. I couldn't see the top of the mountain. Where was it? The bus chugged slowly up the side of the valley; at times I thought the driver might have left the gearbox behind. The winding road was like a stairway to heaven, and we kept going higher and higher. We drove past numerous cyclists who were struggling to cycle up the steep road. They had their jerseys unzipped and wide open leaving a trail of sweat behind them like snails. Every single one of them looked like they were suffering badly and had excruciating pain written all over their face. Would I really have to cycle up this road at the end of the event to find the finish line? Yes, yes I would!

The towns down below in the valley got smaller and smaller as an odd puffy white cloud approached. The main road we had turned off had become a small line with tiny moving dots for cars. Feeling giddy with nerves I was genuinely terrified of the event I had signed up to. I desperately tried to put my fear out of my mind and focus on the wonderful location I was in. I knew it was too late for a dose of doubt, there was nothing I could do about it. My bike had been shipped over from Ireland and was being delivered to my hotel later that day. There was no way I could back out, that would be cowardly. I would just have to suck it up and cycle the route.

Unfortunately, as much as I tried I just couldn't stop my head going off into a spin. I was panicked about what would happen if I did not make the cut-off time set by the organizers? How would it feel to be forced to abandon because I was not able to go fast enough? What if everyone else finished and not me? Oh my gosh! Could I live with that kind of shame? No. No I could not. Potentially I might have to move to a new country out of embarrassment. My mouth went dry, sweat was trickling down my back and my hands were clammy. Silently inside my head I was screaming for help and wondered what the hell I was doing there.

In the months prior to departure I thought my training was "top notch." I had been out in the wind and rain in January. I was following a strict training plan apart from all the days I missed. (Oops!) I promised myself that I would make them up but somehow something else always got in the way. I thought I was great though; I had never before cycled consistently through the winter and was sure that counted as double the effort. (They don't.) Feeling like a lean mean cycling machine, I thought I was more than ready to tackle the mammoth climbs that I had seen on the Tour de France.

In hindsight and reality I wasn't ready at all. I was so ill-prepared I am embarrassed to think about it. Not only was I not fit enough, but my cycling kit was also all wrong too. Half of my stuff was from the supermarket special aisle on Thursdays and the other half was old and a bit shabby. I looked like I had been dressed from a bargain basement bin.

When we arrived in the town I went for a little walk around to try and clear my head, but it made matters even worse. I was mortified when I saw the slick style of the other eight thousand riders. Not only were they suited and booted in high-end Lycra with expensive logos, but they had amazing physiques and looked like professional athletes. They also had shiny, super expensive bikes and sparkling clean white cycling shoes topped off with slick stylish sunglasses. They looked like they had come straight from a photoshoot for a cycling magazine. My lovely red and white bike that I was so proud of by comparison was an entry level road bike that was four years old and weighed a tonne. To top it off my sunglasses had cost me €4.99 in the supermarket. I felt foolish as I walked amongst the cycling "Gods." I was mortified by the state of me.

Feeling deflated and rather stupid for entering such a mammoth event I needed a lot of help to get my head back in the game and forget about everyone else. I had to stop comparing myself to them. We were all there to cycle our own race and that included me. I had a great idea: I needed a mascot to get me through the event, something that I could call on to give me a little boost if things got too tough for me. I wanted something that symbolizes strength, endurance, tenacity and bravery but also is regarded as the underdog.

I chose to be inspired by the Giant Tortoise!

As you know, my trip to the Galapagos Islands was not long before I departed for France. The giant tortoises that were native to the islands had left a lasting impression on me. I was truly fascinated by the wrinkly, slow and majestic creatures.

They were gorgeous in their own, incredibly unique way. I found them to be inspiring and courageous, while plodding along at their own pace. The guide in the sanctuary had explained to me that tortoises are content and at peace on their journey, they just get on with life even though the odds are stacked heavily against them. He told me how tortoises must fend for themselves; they didn't have any parental care. The mother lays her eggs on a beach, covers them over and leaves her babies to fend for themselves. Over time they hatch instinctively to begin their adventure. Unfortunately, Galapagos hawks eagerly sit waiting above the nest, spying on their easy prey. It's heartbreaking to think that the little hatchlings, barely out of their shell, get gobbled up. The poor little things! I was so upset when the guide told me that, but he assured me that most of the tiny tortoises make it to the sea. Instinctively they know how to find the ocean and away they go. The start of a 100-year journey for many.

Somehow, tortoises have kept going. They continue to strive and thrive. They return years later to the very same beach to lay their own eggs and the cycle continues. I loved everything about them and their story of perseverance. They were a very fitting totem for me.

Sitting in my hotel room the night before the Marmotte, I was trying to calm my nerves by examining the route map one last time. I would do my damnedest to overcome the challenge the way I had overcome everything in my life. I would simply get up in the morning, get on with it and be a Giant Tortoise. I would get around the route and finish by any means. I was prepared to crawl on my belly if I had to. I planned to get over each mountain, one at a time and then I would worry about the next part. I assured myself that I would survive the day and complete the route no matter how long it took me. I would also do my utmost to enjoy the journey while seeing a brand-new part of the world. I also tried to remind myself that as an extra bonus I would be out in the sun all day topping up my Ecuadorian tan and meeting lots of fit men on bikes along the way.

"The race is won by the rider who can suffer the most."

-Eddie Merckx

Chapter 11
La Marmotte
France 2014

On the 4th of July 2014 at 7:30am the corral I was shoved into like a sardine opened. Thousands of cyclists poured out into the town of Bourg d'Oisans, clambering and elbowing each other out of the way. Crashing in their haste, some fell over. Like the little turtles you could say they were gobbled up. Unlike many of the others, I kept my cool and exited safely; my first hurdle was complete.

As I glided along the first kilometre I pretended that I was a pro cyclist heading off to complete my very own Tour de France. There were crowds of locals and cyclists' friends lining the main street. The atmosphere was electric as they were clapping and cheering loudly while waving us off. I will never forget the sound of large cow bells ringing which spurred me on as I cycled down the road. I felt like a rock star on wheels. Even though my cycling club buddies were a little ahead of me already, I wasn't going to panic or get upset that they were faster than me. Besides, I had something they didn't, an inner giant tortoise. My round trip of the Alps had begun, and I was going to cycle full circle.

The first climb was really daunting. I was in the Alps after all and really didn't know what to expect in terms of difficulty. I was cycling into the unknown and would just have to follow the road no matter how it unfolded. I was doing OK until I saw a signpost that said there was another 27 kilometres to go to reach the top. My goodness, what the heck was I going to do? There were hundreds of cyclists behind me so I couldn't turn back and ride in the other direction to them. I would stick out like a sore thumb. Plus, I had only cycled five kilometres to the signpost and thought that perhaps given the expense of the trip I should at least try to get to the top of the first peak!

While the route was easy to follow, I didn't like that I could see thousands of cyclists miles ahead of me. They were tiny moving dots, far away in the distance high up into the valley, which made me feel somewhat inadequate.

My inner tortoise kindly reminded me, tortoises are not known for their speed but their incredible endurance. I just needed to keep moving forward at my own pace.

France was just stunning in July. The countryside was flooded in sunshine and the mountain air was crisp and clean. While the Alps were nowhere near as high as the Andes they stretched as far as I could see and then some more. While the route was tough I was very glad to be distracted by nature which made me momentarily forget about my suffering. From the corner of my eye I could see some goats grazing in the meadows, they were side by side with wildflowers, bees and other insects doing their pollinating jobs with finesse and grace.

It was a struggle to get up the mountain but thankfully the road quality was perfectly smooth as it meandered through the greenery, following the natural twist and turns of the landscape. As for me, all I had to do was follow the line of cyclists ahead of me who continued upwards like ants on a mission. In the distance I could see numerous snow-capped peaks; I thought it was funny to see snow in July and had a little chuckle to myself as I imagined snowmen having a beach party. Unbeknownst to me, later in the day I would be cycling on those peaks.

All around me were other cyclists, who like me were huffing and puffing. It would have been nice to be able to talk to them but there was no way I could string a sentence together and cycle at the same time. Thankfully one by one the kilometres passed. Admittedly, some passed very slowly.

When the summit finally came into my sight I was so relieved. I really wanted and needed to get off my saddle and have a little break. My back was sore, I was drenched in sweat, and I was knackered too. I wondered if a lie down would be out of the question at the top. For good measure, I was also dehydrated and starving. Even though I looked and felt a wreck, I was very glad that I had made it to the first summit and was still in one piece.

As a group we had hired a support vehicle which was a lifeline. I was so relieved to see it parked at the top. As I walked towards it I recognised some very familiar cycling jerseys too. Hallelujah, some of my club friends were there too and it turned out, they had arrived not that long before me. They kindly reassured me that I was doing great and was on schedule to make the cut-off in time.

Climbing into the back of the van I pulled out my massive support bag which contained enough food to feed a family for an entire week. I was not entirely sure what I might want to eat on the day so I brought everything I could think of just in case. I also had two changes of clothes in the bag as well as girlie bits like a hairbrush and mirror. (I wanted to look good in my photos!)

Like a wild animal I devoured one of my many bread rolls which was filled with French ham and cheese. I was famished. We had eaten a huge breakfast hours ago, but my stomach must have forgotten as it was begging to be filled. It was just what I needed after my first arduous climb, that, and a restroom!

While all around me men were taking nature breaks freely I preferred to wait until I could find an actual loo. There was just too big an audience at the summit, and I am a bit of a lady when I want to be. I could wait.

Jumping back on my bike, it was time for my first big downhill Alp style. I may have gone down Death Road in Bolivia, but this was an entirely different ball game. There were crowds to navigate, speed, gravity, skinny road bike wheels, and very technical bike handling skills were required. On the bright side, fear of such a steep descent funnily enough helped me to momentarily forget about my bladder.

I had to concentrate fiercely as I navigated hairpin after hairpin, (tight turns), for the first few kilometres, until eventually the road straightened up a little. I went downhill continuously for 11 kilometres, and I could not wait for it to end. Our downhills in Ireland are fun but are nowhere near as technical or long as the ones on the continent. Plus, I know the roads at home and feel much more confident on them. However as I had no idea what lay around the next corner, and I was on the "wrong" side of the road, naturally I braced myself for the worst.

I felt frozen on the bike, gripped by fear. I was squeezing my inner thighs tight into the cross bar for extra sturdiness. While I could not see my face I'm sure panic was written all over it. I was pulling my brakes so hard that the pads were practically melting onto the wheel rims. I simply had to overcome my fear and let go of the brakes otherwise I would lose too much time from being a slowcoach and potentially be late for the cut-off. I needed to call on my tortoise mascot, it was time to be a new-born hatchling and run as fast as I possibly could for the beach.

When I went faster it turned out descending was exhilarating and nerve-racking all at once, but I did it. I have no recollection of the scenery from that section as I was otherwise engaged and hanging on for dear life. It was impossible to notice anything other than the tarmac in front of my face. My first Alpine descent eventually was complete. I was upright and alive, my mission was accomplished. Arriving in the town of St Colomban-des-Villards I spotted public toilets in the main square. While there was a big queue for it I was more than happy to line up. It would be worth it to use an indoor restroom, wash my hands and be nice and comfortable for the next leg of the route. The thought was pure bliss.

Unfortunately, my bliss was completely shattered in an instant. It was by far the worst bathroom I have ever endured in Europe. It was a disgusting outhouse in the middle of a beautiful town. If you had told me it once was a pigsty and the pigs left due to the inhumane living conditions I would have believed you. There was a hole in the floor, while far more hygienic in that situation than an actual porcelain bowl, it made me wish I had just gone in the field at the top of the summit. I have been all over the world to some of the poorest places known to man and endured some harsh toilet conditions which you make allowances for when traveling. I'm not precious in any way when I backpack.

However I had never come across anything like this in Europe - we have standards! How was this allowed to happen? A dirty, disgusting, swamp pit in France is not what I expected. There was no sink or lovely vanity unit with a mirror as I had imagined. I had to wipe my feet on the way out of the cubicle and my tummy retched from the stench. I could not wait to breathe fresh air again. My goodness, I love France, but that needs to be sorted out. Surely there are EU regulations to cover such a travesty. Even though I didn't enjoy using the facilities, I was glad to be comfortable again and that was the most important thing.

The Col du Telegraphe, the second big climb on the route, was up next. A Belgian cyclist who was riding beside me on a flat section was lovely and chatty. It was so nice to have a very pleasant conversation with someone else. We were both misplaced from our respective friends and were glad to have each other's company for a little motivation.

Casually, and being a very helpful guide, he took time to point out our next destination. I nearly fell off my bike. There, straight up in the air, was a fortress, Fort du Telegraphe, rising high into the sky, a sight to behold that would take your breath away. I could just about make out the imposing stone fortress walls surrounding it. Precariously perched on the top of a mountain, it looked as if it had grown out of the ground like a beanstalk in a fairy tale. Bending my head as far back as I could to see all of its glory, the fort was beckoning me to come closer.

Even though I was tight on time, I slowed up for a brief moment to take it all in. I had never seen anything like it before. The last few months I had tried to work on my bike skills and fitness yet had given very little regard or thought to what I would see and who I might encounter while on the trip. I never imagined I would be cycling along a road, looking up at a fortress built two centuries ago, in a beautiful valley surrounded by amazing people on bikes.

I knew that climb would be challenging but I was also sure that my tenacity and sheer stubbornness would get me to the top. It had to! I couldn't and wouldn't let the route get the better of me. Taking a deep breath I dug deep into my soul and put my inner resources on red alert. Strength! Determination! Are you ready? Whether they were or were not I had to get going, after all the clock was ticking...

In the blistering midday sun my Belgian friend and I began our daunting climb. I tried to keep chatting to him to keep my mind distracted, but he was just that little bit stronger than me. As much as I wanted to stay with him, I had to let him go ahead of me. It wasn't far, it was only a few meters. He was so nice to me; on sharp corners I could see him looking back over his shoulder to check that I was there. I felt safer and happier on that climb due to having a "friend."

The road zig zagged steeply up the side of the mountain, up and up and up some more. Like tiers on a cake, I could see most of the levels above and below me. Much to my joy, I could also see hundreds of cyclists moving slowly along on the lower roads. It was comforting to know that even though I was a "tortoise," I was not the slowest rider.

The towns below in the valley became smaller and smaller as the fortress in the air and the clouds got closer and closer. My Belgian friend started to struggle and dropped back to my pace. United once again, I was so glad to have him beside me for chats and motivation. Slowly, slowly we followed the beanstalk all the way up to the fortress in the air.

Much to my joy, finally we turned the last corner and rolled over the line that was spray painted on the road announcing the end of the climb. My Belgian friend and I arrived alive, even though we were both a little broken physically. We hugged, high fived and thanked each other profusely for being there. I don't think I would have reached the top if it hadn't been for him.

Unfortunately, it was time for us to part ways. We each had to find our support vehicles, refuel, and reset ourselves for the next half. He wanted to wait for his friends to arrive while I was the opposite. I needed to eat and get going as soon as possible. I felt that every minute counted, and I could not afford to hang around. I really wished that we could have stuck together for the next leg of the route but sometimes you just have to be brave and go it alone.

Stumbling around on my shaky legs I found my support van once again and pulled out my Mary Poppins bag of endless edible delights! Our van driver told me that all the others from my group were way ahead of me. I was lagging behind and needed to get a move on. Shit! I was still only at the halfway point; I had another big descent to overcome and there were still two mammoth climbs ahead. They were both going to be harder than the two I had already conquered, and goodness knows they were bloody tough. I wondered how the hell would I make it through the rest of the route and make the cut off in time.

I am sure tortoises experience rough waters and occasionally have to deal with harsh tides. I kept telling myself: "This too shall pass," tough times come, and they go. If tortoises could avoid extinction then I could get around a bike ride. While at the time I thought I was out of my comfort zone, in reality, all I had to do was dig a little deeper in my soul. I had plenty of experience in overcoming adversity and pain which I could call upon in tough times.

I grabbed my bike and decided to just go for it on the next downhill. I zipped up my jersey and pedalled over to the edge where the downhill road began. Pausing for a moment, I took a deep breath, said a quick prayer to anyone in heaven who cared to listen. I gritted my teeth and bravely let my wheels roll over the edge. My bike instantly picked up speed and took me rapidly down off theTelegraphe.

Unbeknownst to me, there was a professional photographer hiding around a corner, who was there to take photographs of the cyclists in full action mode. He snapped the most wonderful photos of me bombing downhill on my bike looking like a pro cyclist. I was surprised when I saw him but somehow managed to give him a great big smile. He had billboards up with his website address on it, so the next day I was able to find and purchase my snaps online.

My photographs were stunning! I was smiling brightly and looked high on life while gliding downhill on my red and white bike. There were snow-capped peaks in the background and dainty yellow buttercups in the foreground. It was such a great action shot and one that I treasure. I feel that photograph summed me up. While there was pleasure, pain, highs and lows on the event, I was getting on with it and smiling all the way.

Onwards, my little bike and I rolled through the ski resort of Valloire, which was very pretty in the height of summer. The sun was shining so brightly, highlighting the colourful flower boxes which were bursting with red geraniums. Flowers hung from every available window ledge on the large wooden hotels and restaurants that lined the main street. Cycling through the town the smell of fresh croissants wafted through the air and drifted to my nose. For just a moment, the smell of warm, buttery bread made me forget all about cycling. I was sure the croissants were trying to tempt me to quit my journey and eat the whole lot of them instead. My tummy gave a nice big gurgle in solidarity with the croissants. Even though I had just eaten at the top of the Telegraphe, I felt hunger pangs rumbling in my stomach. They smelt so irresistible, I have to admit, the temptation to stop nearly got the better of me. I was licking my lips and was trying to convince myself that five minutes wouldn't hurt.

Reluctantly I had to snap myself out of my aromatic trance. I simply had to remain focused on the task in hand and get to the cut-off. The only way I could bribe myself to keep going was to promise myself that I could eat as many croissants as I liked the next day. The deal was struck and in case you're wondering, I ate four croissants the next day!

I didn't notice at first, but the road was meandering slowly but surely up and up and up again. When I looked up, high into the valley ahead, once again I could see the stronger cyclists who were just little dots moving far in the distance. I was very envious of them; they were at least an hour ahead of me and clearly they were not under any pressure to reach the cut-off. Reality knocked very loudly on my helmet and reminded me in no uncertain terms, that I was on a challenge, and it was each person for themselves. I needed to stop comparing myself to others and ride my own race. After all, I was now on the highest peak of the day, one of the highest in Europe for that matter, how could it possibly be easy?

Even though I tried not to, I began to feel very anxious. The mountain was huge, and the other riders were so high up, practically in the clouds. The climb looked gruelling, and I had no idea how long it would take me. My thoughts started to turn to failure and self-deprecating words crept into my mental vocabulary. For a moment my head was completely out of control.

I had to get out of the negative hole I was digging for myself. There was absolutely no point beating myself up. There was no other way forward but to "suck it up." After all there was no turning back, the route was a great big circle so either way I was screwed. My inner tortoise shouted loudly, "just keep moving forward."

Turning the pedals I kept on going and much to my surprise it wasn't as hard a climb as I thought it would be. It was actually quite manageable. It was long and sweeping rather than steep and short. Pottering along it suddenly dawned on me that I was overtaking people. I never in a million years expected that to happen. I wondered if perhaps they had pushed themselves too hard too early? I knew that it wasn't because of my incredible cycling prowess, but it certainly looked like slow and steady was winning the race after all.

Higher and higher I went until snow patches started to appear on the mountain. I loved seeing the great big splotches that were sporadically dotted along the side of the road. They got thicker and thicker the higher I went. I really wanted to play in the snow, or at a minimum throw a snowball at someone. However the air temperature was rapidly plummeting, so it was best to keep moving. Powering on through my fatigue I could see cars and vans parked up ahead in the distance. I was sure that must be the top, there would be no other reason for them to be there. All I had to do was get to the cars and I would have three of the four peaks over and done with. My little legs shouted "Yippee!"

My anxiety faded away, in fact I was feeling super smug and rightly so. I was doing great and was happy with my efforts. It was about 4pm at that stage and I still had just over 2 hours before cut-off time. My only concern was my stomach which was rumbling very loudly. I was burning through calories at a ridiculous rate and needed a roast beef dinner with all the trimmings. Even though I had some sweets in my back pocket I didn't dare take my hands off the handlebars for fear of falling off. My gut would just have to wait until I reached my supply bag in the van. I also hoped that when I finally caught up with the support vehicle that some of my gang might be there too. Even though I had chatted to lots of other people on the day I missed my friends and wondered if they were missing me!

The last two kilometres of the climb to the top of Galibier were so difficult. Oh my gosh it was ridiculously steep. The climb went from being manageable to leg breaking. Goodness it was relentless, I was really struggling to stay upright on my bike. I was grinding my pedals with all my might and had my head down, so that, would you believe, I never noticed that I cycled straight past our support van which was parked in a field to my right. It turned out that vehicles are prohibited from the top of the Galibier. Instead, they are diverted through a tunnel which cuts under the mountain peak. People must park their vehicle below the summit and walk from there to the top. This meant that all the support vehicles had set up camp in a large car park before the actual top of the climb. Even with so many cars and vans stopped there I never thought to lift my head and look at what was going on. I was in too much pain to be bothered thinking about them to be honest. In many ways I am glad I missed them, after all, who stops for lunch when you still have 2 kilometres to go to the top? I would never have been able to start again on that ridiculous gradient.

The last 2 kilometres of that climb were sickening. I mean it. I was so ill-prepared for such a steep section at high altitude. The air was becoming significantly cold and thin from being so high above sea level but that wasn't my only problem. Oh my gosh, I thought my kneecaps were going to explode off my legs as I was having to push my pedals so hard to stay upright. I felt like I was climbing straight up the side of a wall.

Exhausted and hungry, the only way for me to get through the last leg was to count the telegraph poles on the side of the road. Each one became a landmark for me. My focus was getting to one post and then on to the next. I was taking baby steps, but I was getting small wins along the way. I kept my focus on the posts but from the corner of my eye I could see cyclists' feet walking along the road. They were pushing their bike up the hill, beaten by the gradient. I could have given in and joined them, but there was no way on earth I was going to walk. No matter how slow I was going, I managed to stay upright on my bike. Powered on by bullish determination, grunting and swearing loudly at times from the pain, I really did not care who heard me. Pulling harder and harder on my handlebars, I dragged myself and my bike up the road. My legs were burning and my whole body was crying for mercy. It felt like my heart was going to burst from exertion and my eyeballs might fall out from the pressure of squeezing every muscle and trying to breathe. It was murder. Worse than that in fact! Sweat was pouring down my face, I was huffing and puffing while still counting the poles. It was working. The telegraph poles went past one by one, slowly but surely the 2 kilometres of hell got shorter and shorter.

The finishing line was drawing closer and closer. I could see the last one on the curve of the summit. I just had to get to it. My heart rate increased with trepidation and excitement as the top was almost in reach. I navigated my way around the walkers and cyclists who were wobbling all over the road. I was going to get there, one way or the other, no one was going to get in my way. Just a few metres left...

I was talking to myself, frantically telling myself to just keep pedalling, grunt some more, push through the pain and give it one last effort. The top was seconds away. I could see the people with cameras and bikes leaning up against a wall. I was hypnotised by them. I shifted attention to another bike that was just ahead of me and kept telling myself to follow it. Shouting loudly at myself one last time "Come on! You got this."

My bike rolled over the arc of the summit, all of a sudden my legs were spinning freely as the tension on my pedals eased. My beautiful bike and I made it. Thankfully both of my kneecaps were still intact, and I was breathing. Phew!

Tortoise tactics triumphed yet again. Stepping off my bike at the top was simply the best feeling I have ever felt in all my life. The relief and gratitude of arriving in one piece brought tears of joy to my eyes. I was an emotional wreck, I felt like I had just arrived home from battle; I was so happy and delighted to be with other people who all felt the same as me. It was so exciting to be there, positivity reeked through the air. Everyone was a hero including me.

Standing at the highest peak of the day feeling so proud of myself, it had made every ounce of pain and suffering worthwhile. My aches and hunger instantly disintegrated and thankfully my body recovered quickly from the torture it had gone through.

I couldn't wait to have my picture taken at the top. Excitedly, I handed my phone to another cyclist who was willing to be my photographer. My little bike and I stood proudly in front of the landmark signpost denoting that we were at 2642 meters above the sea while looking and feeling fantastic. Enjoying my photo shoot, another cyclist warned me not to waste too much time up there. I would get cold. He strongly advised me to wrap up for the descent, it was going to be a long way down. While I wanted to bask in all my glory, he was right. The route was by no means finished and the clock was ticking. I still had to cycle back down the valley to the town where my day had begun and after that I still had to face another arduous climb. I was so wrapped up in my moment of glory that I completely forgot about the final stage. Coming back to reality my stomach gave a very loud gurgle to remind me it also needed food.

Looking around I hoped to see some familiar faces and most importantly my support vehicle. I really needed a crusty roll from my bag since all I had with me were my last few sweets in my pocket. Where was my group? I knew I was slower than most of them and was lagging behind but surely someone else was at the top. Nope, no one. I was wondering to myself if they had legged it with my food or had I misheard the instructions the night before?

My stomach gurgled loudly once again and then, just for an added test to my day, I suddenly got a "kick" in the lower abdominals. It was a massive cramp of the girlie kind. Mother nature had decided there and then that it was my time of the month. Seriously, the day was tough enough as it was, I really did not need that to be thrown at me too. I pleaded with mother nature for some mercy but that didn't work. Her mind was made up and that was that. I could have cried and eaten my body weight in chocolate for comfort.

While I love being a female there are some added "joys" you have to contend with which are especially difficult to deal with when you try to be a sports star. It's not easy and it certainly was horrific timing for me on that day. I was so tired and hungry; I really needed a hug and to find a toilet. (Preferably a nice one that would meet European safety standards!) I was emotional and irritable about the situation, I also needed to find the damn van. Where the heck was it? I wanted my food bag; I desperately needed my personal items and I also wanted to swallow the copious amounts of painkillers I had packed "just in case."

The other problem I was also faced with was another very long and technical descent. There was no way I could safely pull into a tavern to use the facilities even if I saw one. Worrying about time, or rather the lack of it, I decided I had better just keep going and get to the cut-off point. Perhaps the van would be there? Maybe then I could "relax" and sort myself out. There was 50 kilometres to cycle to the timing mat. If I went hell for leather I could easily get there in under two hours. All going well I would cross the timing mat with a few minutes to spare. After that there was only 14 kilometres uphill to the finish line. Easy!

Feeling extremely uncomfortable and sorry for myself obviously works wonders for my cycling ability. Departing the summit I whizzed downhill like a pro. I took corners at speed and followed "the line" of the road. I even leaned into the sharp corners and tilted my body weight to the inside so that I was able to go through them faster. (I didn't know I was able to do that!) There was no time to be precious or scared. Whizzing past others, navigating the turns and bumps on the road I was completely in the moment. Time was of the essence and while I wanted to soak up the scenery, there was no way I was lifting my head. Only the road ahead existed. When I reached the long flat road, I absolutely belted along it overtaking everyone in my path. My tortoise was on a mission and was not taking any prisoners.

I was possessed! I think I left my sanity on the top of the Galibier. I can't blame my hormones on that one, it was like there was an inner demon in me that was in the driving seat. I was screaming at the other cyclists to get out of the way as I bulldozed past them. They were pottering along, which I couldn't understand. They all needed to make the cut off too but didn't seem to care. Unlike me, I was a mad woman on the loose. There was no way I was slowing down for anything or anyone. I just wanted to get to the cut off timing mat, find the van, change my clothes, eat and use a loo, then normal service could resume!

Finally I came to the big roundabout outside Bourg d'Oisans and turned right into the town. Along with groups of other cyclists, once again I headed up the main road which was lined with hundreds of supporters who were cheering loudly at the steady stream of cyclists. Both sides of the road were shoulder to shoulder with friends and families who were clapping and egging us on to get to the cut off. Even though I was absolutely hanging at that stage, I was pushed on by their energy, cheers and wonderful "Allez! Allez! You can do it!" signs.

Digging deep once again I found even more speed from somewhere in my reserve tank. I could see the cut off mat just ahead of me. I got up out of the saddle and sprinted with all my might to reach it. The crowd went wild as myself and other cyclists rolled over the official timing chip. When it beeped loudly to confirm my arrival I thanked my lucky stars for getting me there in one piece.

I had reached the bottom of the fourth climb, the Alpe d'Huez, in record time from the top of the Galibier. It took me just 1 hour 26 minutes to get there with an average speed of 29 kilometres an hour. That was blooming good going considering I had already been on my bike for 9 hours at that stage. I zoomed over the timing mat at 17:55pm, some twenty minutes ahead of cut off time.

As soon as I crossed the line, I jumped off my bike and ditched it in a hedge. Some spectators were trying to pat me on the back, but I had an errand to run. I needed the toilet. I ran across the busy road, sprinting in fact into a nearby campsite. It is funny how some words translate no matter what language you use. I'm not usually one for globalization but on that day I was super glad of it. Thank goodness for big brand names like McDonalds, Coke and Tampax!

The campsite owner was also a woman and much to my delight she was willing to help me. I was so relieved to talk to her as she had a lot of sympathy for me and understood the problem. Ushering me towards the lady's toilet she was so nice until she duly asked me to pay her one Euro for her help. While I was annoyed with that, at the same time I was grateful and wanted to hug her for rescuing me.

While I was freshened up I still wanted to change my clothes and eat the entire contents of my bag in the van. Except there was still no sign of our support crew and vehicle. To this day I have no idea where they were. Much to my upset, I had no choice but to forget about them and yet again on my grand tour, I had to "suck it up."

I was so hungry and weak that I felt like I might pass out. Walking back across the road to find my bike I was unbelievably lucky to spot a supporter in the crowd who belonged to my cycling club, Dan. He was on holidays in the area and had come to cheer us on. He even had the foresight to bring a fuel station with him too. I told him my woes and much to my delight, he kindly pumped Cola and energy bars into me to get me through the last leg. He had participated in the event a few years before and was very sympathetic to both my plight and leg pain. He reassured me that the hard work was done and all I needed to do was one last climb and then I could relax. It sounded so simple when he said it. I loved his pep talk and faith in me, even though I knew he was lying through his teeth. There was no way the last climb was going to be easy.

There was just fourteen kilometres between me and the finish line at the top of the Alpe d'Huez. Me and my inner tortoise were finally headed home. I couldn't wait to arrive at the finish line, collect my medal and get off my bike. Thanking Dan for his kind words and sugar injections, I had to get going. However, due to my extended break, my body had seized up. I was so stiff and sore Dan had to help me to throw my leg over the crossbar. The pain was excruciating, I felt like both my hips were dislocated. My first revolution on the pedals nearly killed me but thanks to Dan giving me a big push off, I was on my way to the finish line.

The Alpe d'Huez was another agonizing zig zag up the side of a mountain face. While I started off enthusiastically that feeling only lasted for about thirty seconds. I was so done with the Marmotte and wondered why they could not have put the finish line at the bottom of this iconic climb? Whose genius idea was it to have it at the top?

It took me two hour and a half -hours to crawl up 14 kilometres at a tortoise pace. Mind you it does average out at 8% incline, so it was a mega challenge. The scenery was lovely though when I did manage to look at it, each sharp corner offered a vast view all across the Alps. Unfortunately as it was so late in the day, the road had reopened to traffic and there were tons of cars and campervans to navigate making it even tougher. At least, given the size of the event, I was not alone. I was amongst a handful of tired and weary cyclists who like me were struggling up to the finish line on their last legs.

At one point I stopped on a corner to take a picture but somehow between taking my phone out of my pocket and lining up my panoramic shot I broke down into floods of tears. It was just a mixture of self-pity and hunger but at the time it felt like I had the weight of the world on my shoulders. Through my sniffles I swore that I was going to sell my bike as soon as I got home and was never going to cycle again. However, despite the pain, agony and tears I never walked with my bike. I cycled the entire way. My endurance gave me some comfort as I watched numerous people pushing their bikes while trying to walk in a straight line. One by one I passed by them upright on my bike.

Many of the cyclists who had already finished were flying past me going downhill with their medals proudly displayed around their necks. Some shouted "Allez" as they passed, trying to motivate me, but in all honesty I was so beaten at that stage that I just couldn't bear listening to them. I know they were well meaning. However, when you are at the end of your tether and grumpy it was just too much for me to take. I will admit to telling them to "Fu*k off" under my breath. I even called them "smug bas***ds and show-offs!" Not to their face, obviously. Besides they were going so fast downhill they would never have heard me even if I screamed at the top of my lungs.

My shorts were chafing me, in fact all my clothes were uncomfortable. Throughout the day they had been wet with sweat and then dry. I felt quite sick and completely miserable. My neck and shoulders were burning too from hanging over the handlebars. My posture had also gone on strike, and I was sure I was swaying from side to side. My back was crippled and screaming with fatigue. No doubt my facial expression told the story perfectly well. In a nutshell, I was completely wrecked. My lack of training, experience, technical handling skills, and ill-fitting cycling kit had made for a most gruelling and punishing day out on my bike.

All I could do to keep going was trying to imagine my medal waiting for me, hanging on the wall, lonely, crying for me to rescue it. I couldn't wait to wear it with pride. Slowly, slowly I turned my pedals.

When the town of Alpe d'Huez finally appeared at the top of the climb I couldn't believe my eyes. Hallelujah! It was getting dark as it was so late in the evening but seeing twinkling lights and the small metropolis gave me a much-needed kick. Hundreds of cyclists were out drinking on the streets with their medals proudly hanging around their necks. They clapped and cheered as I struggled past them. A shell of my former self, draped over the handlebars and in a complete state, I desperately tried to acknowledge them. A man shouted, "just one kilometre to go. Allez! Allez!"

No way! One thousand meters and it would all be over. A firework went off inside me, a sudden power surge came over. My inner tortoise just found another turbo thruster. I jumped up out of the saddle and powered on. I knew that I could cycle that short distance in just a couple of minutes. I was swaying my bike side to side like they do in the Tour de France. In the very last 200 meters I spotted Gar from my group at the finish line. He was cheering and waving at me. Trying to show off to him I went as fast as I possibly could.

The crowds went wild (in my head.) The TV commentators (also in my head) were astounded by my performance, coming in for the final dash and taking the yellow jersey, "she has done it!"

Everyone was clapping and cheering shouting, "Allez! Allez! Allez!" (In my head.) They were all there to see me cross the finish line, take the gold, win for Ireland, be an inspiration for them all. The truth is, the finishers area was shutting up shop, there were just a few beat-up people like me dragging themselves over the finishing line. There were no hordes of people or any sort of fanfare. I didn't care; I had come full circle like all surviving tortoises do. I passed under the inflatable golden arch and crossed the finish line. My own personal Arc de Triomphe. Done and dusted, I felt absolutely delighted, elated and completely frazzled. Stepping off my bike, my feet were happy to finally be standing still. I had cycled for just over 11 hours, was in a heap and could not string a sentence together with exhaustion.

I had stuck it out through thick and thin, well really it was more through pain and more pain, however I got there. My inner tortoise had helped me to put one foot in front of the other until we both returned home. I learnt that day that I had the ability to push through tremendous pain and that I was made of strong stuff. Before that gruelling event, I never thought I possessed resilience.

Hobbling over to the medal stand, I bowed my head and allowed the lady to "crown" me Queen of the mountains. Finally, my finishers bling and I were together. I was overcome with emotions and welled up with happy tears. I was so proud of myself for finishing and couldn't help but smile from ear to ear as I posed for my photo.

As the camera clicked immortalising the moment my aches and pain melted away. They were replaced with pride, adrenaline and a huge happy hormone high. In an instant I had changed my mind, there was no way I was selling the bike, far from it.

When I returned home to Ireland, other cyclists told me about numerous, challenging cycling events and "must do" routes around the world. Like the Marmotte, I simply needed to enter the event and make a trip of a lifetime out of it. I listened in earnest as they described all the wonderful places I could go. There were endless possibilities open to me. I could go long distance, short distance, endurance, flat or hilly. It was totally up to me to decide how much of a challenge I wanted to put myself through.

What really stood out for me was that I could choose to travel alone or with friends. If I travelled solo I would be guaranteed that there would be plenty of other likeminded people there to chat and have fun with. Likewise, if I convinced my cycling friends to go with me I could share lifelong memories with them. It was even suggested to me that I should go bike touring. For that, I simply needed to pop some luggage on my bike and head off on an extended road trip anywhere I liked. It was all new to me and instantly, I was hooked on the idea of cycling holidays. I was excited as I vividly imagined all the amazing trips and places around the world I could visit on a bike.

I didn't know it at the time, but my life was entering a whole new phase, one that would bring me to even more exotic and "way out" places. I began frantically researching iconic cycling routes and record-breaking roads. According to cycling magazines there were many "must do" itineraries and routes to complete. My bucket list instantaneously became three times longer than it already was. I had a whole new feeling of purpose, determination and excitement for life. I loved my work and was happy helping others with their wellness, but for myself, I was going to combine my two great passions, travel and cycling. My bike, my passport and me were going to take on the world!

Chapter 12
Hola! Who's coming to Spain? 2015

"What winter training camp are you doing this year, Sinead?"

To be honest, I didn't even know such a thing existed. I had only just found out about all the amazing cycling events around the world. As if that wasn't enough good news, my cycling buddies explained to me that there were cycling training camps I could visit too. What a great idea! When I spoke to more and more cyclists it became apparent that going to a camp was the "in thing" to do. If only I had known, it could have made my life in France a lot easier.

A weeklong, full-on cycling camp was exactly what I needed if I was going to attempt more cycling adventures abroad. While I did get around the Marmotte I really wished that I had been stronger and more prepared, both mentally and physically. I also required a lot more technical bike handling skills and confidence on my bike, especially on downhills. A training camp would definitely help me to improve my cycling ability while giving my passport another much needed trip to the airport.

With some research and more chats, it turned out that cyclists from all over Europe flocked to Southern Europe in March and April to jump-start their fitness and knock off any winter body weight they were carrying. The most popular destinations were Mallorca, mainland Spain, the Canary Islands, South Italy and Cyprus. It's no wonder they were such cycling hotspots, given how lovely and warm they are with sunny skies at that time of year. Perfect for wannabe pro-athletes like me.

My mind was made up, I was going on one. Location-wise, all I cared about was sunshine, but I absolutely wanted to find a cycling camp that included Yoga on the itinerary. If I was going to spend a week grinding my pedals for hours on end, then I definitely wanted lots of stretching to help my tired body to recover as quickly as possible.

I attribute a lot of my good health and fitness to practising Yoga regularly. It has helped my mobility in more ways than one. When I was an infant I suffered a dislocated hip due to an infection and spent a month in traction. There were disastrous repercussions including joint damage in my hip which caused me agony in my teenage growth spurt years. Frequently I cried with the pain as my body tried to grow around my imperfection. The orthopaedic "specialist" I was sent to back then, told me to sit down and do nothing for the rest of my life. Seriously! I was fourteen years old and that was the best solution he could come up with. I was absolutely horrified by his words. In fact his advice truly terrified me, and I wondered what he was prescribing to his other patients.

Even though he was the one with the fancy qualifications and big office, deep in my soul I knew he was completely wrong. Thankfully, my independent streak was starting to flourish and there was not a chance in hell that I was going to follow his orders. While most teenagers rebel and make mistakes, I don't think that anyone could blame me for doing the complete opposite of what he advised. I was not going to sit still and do nothing, how could I? Keeping active was ingrained in me; besides, I didn't want to stop. Instead I continued to climb trees, ride my bike, dance and do gymnastics. I have even run marathons on my wonky hip and it's more than fine. Anarchy at its best! Thank heavens I listened to my gut instinct. Can you imagine me sitting still, seizing up and going bonkers? No way was I doing that. No thank you.

Even though I was only a young teenager, I was adamant that I would find alternative ways to ease my aches and pains and live a "normal" active life. While I found all kinds of movement to be beneficial, overall Yoga has been by far the best pain relief I have ever found. It keeps my damaged hip joint supple and pain-free and helps me to continue being active and healthy. As you know, Yoga was there for me too when I needed internal help over the years too. Yoga makes me slow down, breathe, relax and rejuvenate both my body and my soul. It's the complete opposite to cycling, I found my Ying to my Yang.

Continuing my search for the perfect cycling camp, I found plenty of them that "guaranteed" sunshine, but I couldn't find one that offered a Yoga recovery program too. No such thing existed anywhere. I was really disappointed, and I wondered why no one was thinking of the big picture, since it was so obvious to me that you had to have the two, hand in hand. Instead, the camps were all about hard-core bike rides, with macho and ego-driven training goals. They promoted how they would help their customers to improve their cycling, but there was no mention of the body that was riding the bike! It was just plain bonkers to me that recovery was totally overlooked.

One night, while fast asleep, I was curled up cosy and warm when suddenly my eyes sprang open and out of nowhere I had a lightbulb moment! If I could not find what I was looking for then why not create it? It was brilliant and such a simple idea. I was sure that I couldn't be the only person on the planet that wanted to cycle like a maniac, do Yoga afterwards and have lots of fun with others. Frantically I made a few notes (yes, I do have a pen and paper on my bedside table). Furiously I scribbled down my ideas, plans and thoughts. I tried to go back to sleep but I was so wound up and excited that I turned on my laptop and started my extensive research there and then. I knew exactly what I wanted. I just needed a winning location, great accommodation, top-notch bikes, a few guides who knew the routes, space for Yoga and delicious food!

My mission was very clear. I wanted to help other cyclists who needed encouragement, advice and time to become better riders while looking after their most important asset, their body. I wanted everyone to leave the trip a little more bendy, fit, suntanned and have more confidence in their bike handling skills. I was going to show them that there was a big wide world out there just waiting to be explored on two wheels.

There was one huge, non-negotiable in my plans. The cycling had to be challenging but also there had to be bucket-loads of fun. I didn't want my trip to be some sort of stuffy camp for elite cyclists with egos whose only aim on any given day was to show off. There were already plenty of those types of camps for the "fast guys" to go to. My trip was different. It was going to be for "real people," those who love to cycle but would also like to improve. If anyone wanted a few drinks, to live on ice cream or skip a cycle then that wouldn't be a problem, there would be no judgement.

On numerous occasions I had seen advertisements on Facebook for a cycling camp in Spain, run by an Irish man, Cormac. I was drawn to his ads: maybe it was the algorithms that kept showing them to me or perhaps it was fate but either way I wanted to talk to him. With even more research (admittedly it was mainly cyber stalking) I found out all about him and his new hometown, Velez. It looked and sounded perfect. The location was idyllic. Nestled in the south of Spain, the small, whitewashed town was just a few kilometres from the coast but also in the foothills of a mountain range. The fact that he was Irish too sealed the deal for me. I felt sure he would be much easier for me to approach with my idea, plus there would be no language barrier or cultural differences.

The more I read about him and googled the town, I knew that without a doubt Cormac was exactly the person I needed for a cycling and Yoga collaboration. I had it all worked out, I just needed him to agree! I was already there in my head: as clear as day I was visualising myself cycling in sunny Spain and teaching Yoga outdoors in the evenings to tired and stiff cyclists. In my daydreams, I also included huge dishes of paella with crispy rice stuck to the edges. I was 100% sold on my idea.

I really felt that Cormac and I would be the perfect duo. I was so excited by the thoughts of collaborating with someone else and working for a week in a hot country. It would be a dream come true for me. I hoped that with my charm and wit I could captivate his imagination and he would be mesmerised by my business pitch. Even if he wasn't convinced, one way or another I was going to make my dreams come true and build a business through my passion for travel, cycling and wellness.

As you know I don't hang around in life. The very next morning I picked up my phone and rang him. My heart was pounding with the jitters, and I kept reminding myself that it was OK if he refused my offer. He was only the first person I was touching base with, there were plenty more fish in the sea if he said no.

When the phone began to ring, instantly I started having heart palpitations which went into overdrive when he picked up the phone and said "Hola."

I stammered and stuttered until I finally got my words out of my mouth. Sheepishly I introduced myself and tried to break the ice with small talk, but I got a little flummoxed, panicked and launched straight into my idea. I babbled for a while and repeated myself incessantly but whatever I said something must have hit a chord with him. My gut feeling had been right, just like me he was open-minded and willing to try something new. Thankfully he too saw the potential we had for a niche market. He was easy to talk to and agreed that we should definitely try to make a go of it and see what happened. Before I knew it, we were discussing logistics and dates and ironing out the fine print. That day, out of the blue, a friendship and business were created.

With a lot of background work, marketing and word of mouth we welcomed our first guests in March 2015. I physically met Cormac for the very first time in Malaga airport after some 7 months had passed since our initial phone call. It was a little surreal to be honest. We had spoken many times and had sent each other hundreds of emails but it was a little strange to be standing face to face with him as we were about to embark on a week-long business trip together. I needn't have worried though as soon as we started chatting it felt as though we had been running tours together for years and could read each other's minds. I adored that he was highly organised too and also had a love of charts and checklists. When I saw his colour-coded spreadsheet I had no doubt that we would work very efficiently together.

Checking the monitor in the arrival hall the flights changed their status to "landed." Immediately my palms went clammy, and my heart was skipping beats with sheer terror. Deep down inside me there was just a tiny little hint of excitement but there was far more anxiety and anticipation as I nervously waited for the group to walk through arrivals. I was terrified in case they didn't have fun, or worse, they were no fun!

My mind started to panic and stress about the entire trip. I was worried sick with what would happen if they didn't like the place or the routes. I was hugely concerned in case the routes were not tough enough or worse, that they were ridiculously hard. After all, I had never been to the area and had taken Cormac's word that the region was excellent for cycling, but in reality, I had no idea if that was true! To top off my panic attack, I was apprehensive, worried sick in fact, that someone might have an accident. Worst of all, what if it rained?

Cormac on the other hand was used to ferrying guests around and had all the logistics down to a tee. He was as cool as a cucumber and was taking it all in his stride. I was so glad to have a wing man standing beside me in the airport and I was able to follow his professional lead as he greeted our new arrivals one by one.

Thankfully, all of my fears were proven to be futile. Cormac and his staff were brilliant guides. He was sincere and helpful just as I hoped. He assured the group that he would build up their fitness and progressively make the routes harder as the week went on. He was very encouraging to everyone. It didn't matter if they were the strongest or the weakest, everyone was motivated and cared for equally. As for me, I enjoyed being on his team, even if it was just a guest appearance on my part.

Cruise ship, 2007

India, 2008

Snoopy and me

Bolivia, 2010

Bolivia, 2010

La Marmotte, 2014

La Marmotte, 2014

Spain, 2015

Hiking in Myanmar, 2017

Myanmar, 2017

Alto De Letra, Colombia, 2018

The Lost City, Colombia, 2018

High on life

Cuba, 2019

Cuba, 2019

Señor cowboy, Cuba, 2019

Tobacco plantation, Cuba 2019

Snapped Achilles

Gran Canaria, 2020

Bikepacking Spain, 2021

Living the dream

Sooty and me

Living our best life

As promised, the routes did become more and more challenging but in a good way. Unlike the Alps there was no altitude to contend with but there were very long climbs to conquer and enjoy. Thankfully there was no cut-off time either and everyone was able to take the hills at their own pace. All our guests were happy to push themselves out of their comfort zone while knowing at the same time, they didn't have to break any world records. Plus it was a little easier to get to the top of the climbs when there were others who were feeling the same level of pain and enjoyment.

After every spin there was a little celebration over drinks and tapas in the afternoon sun. Funnily enough, everyone enjoyed that part of the day the most. It was a joy to hear their personal stories of how they struggled and overcame their pain to triumph and find pride in themselves for not quitting. I knew exactly how they felt and was secretly thrilled that my guests had pushed their boundaries and were smiling because of it. They were all united in overcoming pain while cycling, and they were forever bound together by group photos at the top of the peaks.

As for Cormac and me, we got on great during the week. Our equal love of being highly organised proved to be our superpower. He was in charge of all things bike-related, and I was in charge of customer care and of all things Yoga. Though the week was busy for both of us, we still managed to have a lot of fun together. We were partners in crime who were both very dependable and solid. What worked best for me was that like myself, he just got on with it and didn't mince his words either. At times I wondered if he was my long-lost twin!

Thank goodness the weather was idyllic that week. It was glorious. Each and every morning we were greeted by blue skies and very pleasant temperatures. Coming from cooler climates the trip was the perfect end to our winter hibernation. Just like me, all the guests felt liberated by throwing off their winter woollies in March. We exchanged them for bright and light summer cycling kits. We all loved feeling the fresh air and sun on bare legs which were very pale from not seeing the light of day all winter. In contrast, Cormac and his Spanish guides were cycling in their full winter kit. They felt it was still too cold to wear shorts and kept reminding us it was only March. We couldn't help ourselves and made fun of Cormac, teasing him that he was no longer Irish if he thought 22 degrees was cold. With his copper red beard and auburn hair he wasn't exactly a typical Mediterranean, yet he was acting as though he was a hot-blooded Latino.

Each evening, before sunset we rolled out our Yoga mats and enjoyed stretching in the warm, fresh mountain air. After hours of cycling, our guests walked into their Yoga class like cowboys with buckled, bowlegs and stiff backs. However, with some help from me and gentle recovery Yoga, by the end of their class they walked out like dancers, all limbered up ready for an evening performance.

It was a joy to teach the classes. Our Yoga studio was a wonderful, spacious rooftop garden with views of the mountains that circled the entire town. Oh my gosh! That's what life is all about if you ask me. There is a saying, that "when you do what you love, you will never work another day in your life." I wholeheartedly agree.

I was lucky enough to teach Yoga outside on the deck of the cruise ship as we sailed the seven seas, which was unbelievably amazing. When I left ship life I never thought in a million years that I would create the same wonderful experience on dry land, but as it turned out, a rooftop in Spain was just as good, if not even better.

For the icing on the cake, we brought everyone to the beach for a sunset Yoga class and fun in the sea. No one needed encouragement to lie down on the sand, relax and listen to the sea as it gently and methodically rolled in and out on the shore. Everyone enjoyed looking up at the blue sky as it changed from blue to orange, purple and grey. It was a wonderful way to finish a hard day cycling for all of us, myself and the guides included. All our guests agreed that they felt revived and brand new from spending so much time outdoors on both their bikes and Yoga mats.

After class most of us ran straight into the cold sea and had a good old splash around. It was blooming cold but at the same time it was super refreshing. (It was March after all.) We were like big kids in the sea, splashing around, squealing and laughing out loud as the waves rolled in wrapping cold salty water around our bodies. While they all got to improve their cycling and fitness that week, I think unbeknownst to everyone they got more benefit from being out in nature, soaking up Vitamin D from the sun, laughing all week and playing with the waves while being carefree. It was a holiday that came with many benefits.

Not only did myself and Cormac prove to be a power duo, but the group got on fantastically well too. Usually there is always "one," but on that trip thankfully I couldn't find them. There weren't any clashes of personalities that I could see. Everyone mingled and enjoyed the other people's company especially over our evening meals together.

During the week drinks were flowing too, with each person enjoying their holiday their way. I never wanted to create a trip where people were expected to behave or act in a certain way. After all, I'm all for individuality and self-expression, and I wanted everyone to be themselves and do whatever they wanted (as long as they were safe). We had so many lovely people on our first trip it made the entire process completely painless for me. Their attendance not only gave me the confidence to arrange the trip annually with Cormac, but it encouraged me to set up luxury Yoga Spa Breaks in Ireland and Majorca too which have been a huge success over the years. After all, why would I stop at one business trip in the sun when I could have multiple?

That one simple phone call opened so many doors for me. Over the years, our numbers grew and grew. We made a few adjustments and changes along the way thanks to feedback from our guests. We even started to welcome elite cyclists on the trip (provided they were fun)! We have three groups daily for different abilities from "supersonic, ride like maniacs" to those who, like me after France in 2014, needed quality cycling time, encouragement and technical help. There have been so many memorable people who have come on the trips, and I am sure there are many more ahead of us. While cycling and Yoga took up most of the day, we also found space in our itinerary for wine tasting, trips to vineyards and fancy restaurants. We also have some very funny stories from each group. Touch wood, so far there has been just one puncture which just had to be me and my bike. There was also one big mishap with numerous bottles of gin on an unexpected rainy day. The whole group got drunk as lords and struggled to cycle the next day!

The group on our inaugural week were all Irish but since that year, we have become more popular than I ever imagined. Cyclists come from near and far to join us, indeed some of our weeks have been like a United Nations conference, with the U.S.A, Canada, Switzerland, Poland and France all sitting at the same table for dinner.

Much to my delight, when I asked the very first group for testimonials, without any coercion, they used words such as fitter, happier and healthier to describe how they felt at the end of the trip. They had got exactly what I wanted to deliver from our weeklong collaboration.

Naturally it was extremely disappointing when Cormac and I had to cancel the trip in both 2020 and 2021. The pandemic was an unfortunate interruption for everyone, but it was out of our control. Like everyone else we just had to put the good times on hold and wait it out. However, we were thrilled when normal service resumed in March 2022.

The fun times returned as myself and Cormac welcomed our guests from all over Europe to our quaint base town in the foothills of the mountains. The two-year break was tough on everyone, but we were delighted that so many previous guests returned to us. Once again we all got to wear cycling shorts and sunscreen in March as we rode along the coast in glorious sunshine. In the evenings we stretched on our Yoga mats and relaxed with good food and drinks. It was as if I had never left, and I felt that I was back in my home from home. As always, the warm breeze was there waiting for me as I whizzed down the side of the mountains at high speed being cheered on by the oranges that were dangling from the trees.

CAMBODIA

Chapter 13
The Killing Fields & wandering hands. Cambodia 2017

My annual cycling and Yoga trip to Spain was firmly established in my calendar along with all my Christmas adventures. In December 2015 for my annual trip of a lifetime I went trekking through the Himalayas, all the way up to Everest Base Camp. The journey into the valley was extremely arduous due to the high altitude. Unlike previous trips, in Nepal I suffered very badly with altitude sickness which made me feel absolutely dreadful. After 6 days of trekking, when I finally arrived at Everest Base Camp (5,360 meters) I was practically crawling on my hands and knees due to an unmerciful headache. Not only that, but I had also vomited several times that morning and continued to feel nauseous all day. I was disoriented and as if all that was not enough, I felt as though my head might spontaneously explode off my shoulders at any moment.

In hindsight my guide should not have let me proceed as many people have died on the trek from the side effects of being at altitude. Thankfully, as you have guessed, I didn't die but, goodness me, it was an extremely tough adventure in more ways than one. A few months before I arrived in Nepal, there was a catastrophic earthquake. The whole country was decimated both physically and economically. Needless to say their tourist industry was on its knees post natural disaster, and to add to their troubles, there was a fuel shortage too. Simply put, tourists were scarce, and livelihoods were gone. With a little research I was assured it was still okay to travel there and decided not to cancel my impending trip. I was more than glad to help and support their economic recovery, however, the trade-off was that there were very few tourists on the route at that time.

Luckily there was a lovely Canadian girl, Mazie, and a Thai man, Sumet, who were both on the same beaten track as me to Everest Base Camp. Like myself, they each had booked a group trek but there were no other tourists on their 10-day tour either. Thankfully the three "groups" joined forces which made the trek much more enjoyable for us all, including the guides and sherpas. We were all very glad of each other's company, especially as we went higher, and the air became thinner. Myself and Mazie had something a little quirky in common too, we were both travelling with a soft toy, our little mascots. She was a huge X Files fan and had a small Mulder and Scully with her, while I was carrying a pocket-sized Snoopy teddy. As you know when I was in France I used an imaginary tortoise mascot to get me around the route. Thankfully for the mighty Himalayas I had the sense to pack something more tangible, my favourite cartoon character in the world, Snoopy. Myself and Mazie giggled as we took photos of our respective mascots along the journey and chatted endlessly about future travels we hoped to bring them on.

Even though the three of us were fit, the trek was tiring. The living conditions were not bad, though they were basic. Having fun and chatting with each other along the way became essential to our success. Even though each of us took a turn at feeling beyond miserable from the altitude, we still managed to encourage one another and make the experience more memorable for each other. Don't get me wrong, in spite of the terrible altitude sickness I loved the trek, especially the incredible scenery.

Trekking through the Himalayas was spectacular and definitely a once in a lifetime, must-visit place if you are ever lucky enough to go there. Along the trek we passed numerous Buddhist stupas that were adorned in brightly coloured prayer flags. It was very comforting to know that both the area and all who travel through it were blessed.

Our journey deep into the Himalayas brought us along the Dudh Kosi river which was fed from the melt water off Mount Everest. Our guide told us that the river was classed as "tame," but it was fierce in my eyes. Even though they wobbled, I for one was very glad to cross over it on rope bridges which were suspended high above the gushing waters.

At times when we were walking along the trail we heard bells chiming and the sound of horseshoes rapidly coming our way. We knew to jump out of the way, because it was a donkey "cargo train" coming through. Each animal was loaded up with supplies and was on the "highway" between towns. As they trotted past us we admired their colourful harnesses and hard work. The donkeys were not in any harm or being mistreated. They were working animals. The odd time when we met them on a rope bridge we just had to back up as there was no way they were stopping or moving over for us!

As we got higher the donkeys were no longer the transportation vehicles. Instead Sherpas would push past us, loaded to the hilt with "stuff." One slightly built man could be carrying six boxes of beer, fruit and veg topped off with a chair. There was no limit to their strength and endurance. Even my sherpa was amazing as he carried his luggage, my bag and other essentials we needed for the trip without complaint for 10 days. While I am small, he was tiny with the strength of an ox.

Along the journey we passed Tengboche Monastery where we stopped and watched the monks playing cricket in their orange robes for a little while. I'm not sure who was winning but they certainly were not going easy on each other. It was nice to see that they are human too and even have a competitive edge. As we continued further, high above the tree line, we saw huge, hairy yaks grazing in the meadows.

It felt like I was in another world up there; in fact it was such a world, one that was quiet, slow and relaxed. All the while as we walked higher and higher and became more remote, we were protected by the highest mountain range on the planet which watched over us. The scenery was spectacular, breath-taking in fact. I had been to the Andes and the Alps, but the Himalayas were so different. They reached high up into the clouds, fooling you into thinking you could see the top. With closer inspection I could see there were even higher points peeking out from behind the fluffy clouds. Every now and again mother nature would politely remind us that we were in her territory. One day we heard a loud rumbling like an earthquake. Our guides pointed out to us, high up on the side of a mountain, an avalanche crashing down the valley. Mazie, Sumet and I looked at each other with wide eyes, all thinking the same thing, was that normal? Our guides and sherpas didn't flinch for a second but the three of us quickened our step to move onwards just in case.

While the scenery was tremendous, I got a very big dose of reality during my visit to the Himalayas, a harsh one at that. Nepal was so poor. We walked past children who were being schooled in the middle of a field. Our guide told us that it was warmer for them to sit out on the grass in the cold mountain air in the depths of December than to sit inside their cold classrooms which were built of stone. I felt so sad as I watched them doing their lessons. It wasn't fair or in any way OK for them to have to endure such harsh conditions. I realised how completely spoiled I had been growing up and actually felt very guilty about my education, especially given all the complaints I had made about it over the years. I had no idea how lucky I was.

At night myself, Mazie and Sumet sat around playing cards by stove burners that were fuelled by dried out yak dung. Unfortunately it was not much use and gave off just a little heat. The locals didn't have any other fuel alternatives given the remoteness of the Himalayan towns. At night the temperatures plummeted so low that ice formed on the inside of the windows.

While my trek was a feast for my eyes it was a very big tug on my heart strings. After my ten-day trek I got to return to Ireland to my luxurious life while they, the locals, remained up there in the mountains living a very tough and meagre existence.

In 2016 my December trip of a lifetime was a little unusual. I ended up staying home in Ireland. It wasn't my first choice of destination if I am honest, but my circumstances had changed. I was in a big romance. I had met someone, and I was mad about him! It took a lot for me to let my guard down and open my heart, but I was glad that I had. I would have liked to travel abroad for Christmas as I was worried how I would manage the darkness, but I was thrilled that there was someone else to consider in the equation. Instead, I stayed home for the festive season and was a social butterfly with my guy. While I hated that we only had limited daylight, I was surprisingly nice to enjoy being home for a traditional Christmas dinner and spending the festivities with my family. It had been a number of years since I had done that, and I know they were glad that I joined them.

My man had commitments of his own, and not one to sit around waiting by the phone, I went to Kerry for a few days on my own. While I enjoyed being in Dublin I was very glad to escape the hustle and bustle of the city and hide away in the national park. I had the best of both worlds, Christmas at home, plenty of food and a solo holiday for my quality "me time."

I couldn't go on a trip and not bring my bike with me. Thanks to some very mild weather I was able to go cycling around the Black Valley and enjoy the scenery the "Kingdom of Kerry" was so proud of. I even hiked up Ireland's highest mountain, Carrauntoohil while I was there. In comparison to Mount Everest it is a mere pimple on the face of the earth, but I enjoyed the summit, nonetheless. Unlike the Himalayas I climbed Carrauntoohil in a few hours and got to spend the night in a very warm hotel afterwards. It actually felt good to support Irish tourism for a change. It was a great reminder that I live in a wonderful country that deserves some love, time and exploration too.

Unfortunately, later in 2017 the shit hit the fan once again for me. While my work was going great, and sport, hobbies and friends were brilliant, there was a huge elephant in the room. Unlike the one I had ignored for years in my past; this one could not be unseen. Things were going from bad to worse in the romance department and while I never wanted to stop trying to make it work, there were other factors that were out of my control. It all went completely pear-shaped and that was that! We broke up and there was not a thing I could do to fix the situation. I felt like I had got a swift kick in the derriere to remind me that life is never plain sailing. I guess someone up in "heaven" decided my life needed another shake-up.

After my "episode" in 2005 I had remained single for a very long time, ten years in fact. You could say I wasn't exactly in a hurry to settle down. However when I did eventually meet someone, it was bliss. I really liked being with a man, but I was also lucky enough to have plenty of time for my life. I still had my cycling club, adventures and trips with friends. On the other hand I also had romantic getaways and a life as part of a pair. It was a great combination in the beginning, and I was madly in love. I couldn't believe my luck; I thought I had hit the jackpot!

I will admit that more than anything I had wanted my totally unrealistic fairytale "happy ending." In my head I had said "yes to the dress" I just hadn't noticed that no one was asking me to marry them. When my hopes were shattered, and I found myself solo again I had to rethink my entire future which I had meticulously planned out. There would be no dress, no honeymoon in the Maldives and no one pledging to love me for better or worse. I had to go back to the drawing board and erase "they all lived happily after."

While I never wanted to be single ever again, whether I liked it or not, I had no choice but to suck it up and get on with it. Life was forcing me to dig deep, yet again, I had to call on my inner strength and walk the line alone. I felt deeply ashamed that it hadn't worked out, I was embarrassed to be in my forties and single. Worst of all I had to put up with people's pity and inane comments like "there's plenty more fish in the sea," which killed me even more than waking up alone.

At least by the time that challenge arose I was aware of my issues and had good self-care tools to look after my mental health. I recognised that some old patterns were doing their very best to bubble back up to the surface and tempt me into a catastrophic head spin. It was an all too familiar feeling and it needed to stop. There was no way in hell I was ever going back to revisit such a dark place. It was OK to be heartbroken, angry and upset with the situation, but it was not OK to let my bruised ego run riot and take over my head. I was very aware that I could slip downhill if I wasn't careful. The danger signs were all there: I was becoming extremely negative, blaming myself entirely for the breakup and was being incredibly hard on myself.

I had to be on my guard every minute of every day of my inner critic who was battling to be seen and heard. Without ignoring or invalidating "her," I acknowledge her numerous complaints and hurt. I reassured her that "we" would be OK in a while. We had to ride the storm, it was just a setback in life and the best was yet to come. Every day I took time to journal my thoughts and feelings to help clear my head. I cycled as much as I could with my friends to forget my upset and did my best to have fun.

As part of my self-care I knew I needed to quit alcohol with immediate effect. Like everything in my life I was drinking by the "all or nothing" rule. Once the decision was made I never, ever gave it a second thought again. People don't believe me that I just stopped one day but I did. I made a promise to myself that I wouldn't let myself spiral out of control and as you may or may not know, alcohol can make you do stupid things. I just didn't need to take that risk! I didn't want to be the one sending drunk text messages in the middle of the night or worse, ringing my ex and telling him what I really thought of the situation. No, I had to be ladylike and take my newfound freedom on the chin. Alcohol had to go, there was no ifs, buts or ands about it. I was glad to stop, actually I needed to stop. It wasn't doing me any good, emotionally or physically. I had a little beer gut that I hated and was very pleased when it melted away. Emotionally, being alcohol free helped me immediately to feel better in myself, I was more rational, and my mood swings evened out. Plus, I was eating better as there were no more hangovers that required greasy, salty food for "soakage."

I even went back to college to keep my brain busy, I studied for a diploma in Life and Business Coaching which was invaluable to me at that time. There was a lot of personal development involved on the course which was no harm at all. I was very open to looking into my soul again and even though I didn't like everything that I found there, I was willing to admit my faults and failures as well as acknowledge my many qualities and strengths. While I was keeping myself busy and my mind occupied, this only helped to distract me in the short term. I needed something bigger!

There was only one thing for it. My heart might have been broken but my passport was not. Doing what I do best I packed my bags (Snoopy too) and jumped on a long-haul flight to Myanmar (Burma) to go find myself, again! I could have done what most people do and go find myself in someone else's arms. However I'm not most people. Rolling out of one bed and into another solves nothing: inevitably you find the same crap there and you're the common denominator. Instead I chose to spend a month solo traveling in December. I even went to Cambodia while I was over that direction. Sure why the heck not?

My month-long trip was just what the doctor ordered. It turned out sunshine, rice and temples were the perfect cure for a broken heart and a bruised ego. I wasn't running away or not dealing with my feelings. It was quite the opposite. I was giving myself time to heal in a positive and healthy way.

I made sure on that trip to take quality time for my annual appraisal which went surprisingly well. Things weren't as bad as I initially thought. When I sat down and weighed up the pros and cons of my new situation I realised very quickly that I was better off being single, "me" again. I had been working to someone else's schedule, giving everything and getting next to nothing in return. It was not a win-win in any shape or form and deep down I knew it all along and it showed. I couldn't control my feelings of frustration with the relationship dynamics and would regularly throw a tantrum which got me absolutely nowhere. Nothing changed. I felt like I was banging my head off a wall and my soul was hurting. I was not being true to myself, settling for less than I deserved and as much as I didn't want to admit it, stronger forces were at work. It was only when we went our separate ways that I suddenly felt like I could breathe again.

The time had come once again to take full responsibility for my own happiness and look after myself. I needed to listen to my inner voice and resurrect the strong independent person I once was. My eastern odyssey was for me, by me! I was relieved that there was no co-dependency. I didn't have to consider anyone else's feelings or schedule, only my own. I was free to be "selfish" and I was excited. I was going to do whatever the hell I wanted for four weeks and enjoy every minute of it. I was also going to take the opportunity to think about my needs, dreams and hopes for my new future. Sure I wanted to be with someone, but it had to be right. In the meantime, more than anything, I wanted my life to involve even more travel, adventure and excitement. I didn't care whether that life was with or without someone else, I knew I would be fine either way.

I had so much fun on my trip and met so many wonderful people that my tears of heartbreak were soon forgotten and turned into tears of laughter. I loved both Myanmar and Cambodia immensely even though they each had their problems. Myanmar was a political hot potato at that time due to numerous human rights violations, and Cambodia was a country with a history of a genocide so hideous it made me retch with disgust. Both countries were equally interesting - alive, fun, amazing, and yet both totally individual, each with their own turbulent past, present and future. I just loved everything about them both from start to finish, especially the local people, their culture and most of all their superb food. I am sure I was Asian in a previous life: I love it there and I feel very much at home and in my element. I could happily live on rice and spices. I fit in too, literally, as you know I'm pint sized, and I adored being at eye level with the locals!

There were some harrowing times on my trip though, especially in Cambodia. I visited the Killing Fields (Choeung Ek) just outside the capital city Phnom Penh. While informative, it was not easy to witness how terrible mankind could be. I got to see first-hand the most vile and disturbing low point of Cambodia's history. While I wasn't a part of it I felt truly ashamed to be a human being. I bawled my eyes out as I listened to the audio guide recount the harrowing actions of the Khmer Rouge. It was unbearable to hear how, in the exact spot where I was sitting in the sun, such sickening acts of violence had occurred just a few decades ago. My soul was so deeply touched by the anguish the victims must have felt in their final moments. I was sure I could hear their cries in every rustle of the trees and feel their pain in the heavy air that circulated around me.

Trying to compose myself and dry my eyes I looked around me. There was a large, glass memorial tower in the middle of the "field" piled high with human skulls, each one had been bashed in with a wooden weapon to end their life. All of those broken skulls used to be someone whose life was brutally cut short. In stark contrast, there was I, in Cambodia on the trip of a lifetime, sitting on a bench in a peaceful memorial site with no real worries. I was happy and healthy with my whole life ahead of me. I had choices, was free to travel and I had plenty of friends and fun in my life. It wasn't the first time I had sat on a bench and contemplated the meaning of life, my life to be exact. As you know, in 2005 I had sat on the bench in that hellhole behind four walls and vowed to change my life for the better. While sitting in the Killing Fields, under a large tree which provided me with much needed shade from the sun I decided that it was time for another intervention.

In the grand scheme of things I had no reason to be upset. I knew that I had been doing great before my romance had started and I would be fine after it. Surrounded by mass graves it was easy to remind myself that our time on earth is short and should not be squandered on pity parties. I had done my crying over the break-up, and it was time to move on to bigger and better things. I had already turned my life around for the better once before, I could do it again. I knew the routine and had more than enough skills to deal with change.

After my upsetting but profound visit to the Killing Field I whizzed around the capital of Cambodia, Phnom Penh, in a tuk-tuk driven by a wannabe rally driver. He certainly knew how to bring me back into the moment as he drove like a maniac through the busy streets. He took corners at great speed, just about missed countless pedestrians and braked so hard I nearly ended up flying out over his steering wheel. I loved every minute of it! I was hanging on for dear life, squealing with joy at the same time while trying to wave to the local children who were pointing and laughing with glee as they saw another European hanging on for dear life in a runaway tuk-tuk.

From the capital I travelled by bus to the north of the country. I was lucky enough to spend five days in Siem Reap where I went to see the archaeological site of Angkor Wat, the biggest religious monument in the world. I was fortunate enough to watch the sun rise over the magnificent temples, and then I duly melted in the mid-day sun as I tried to explore the entire complex in two days.

A very big part of my trip was also about self-care, fun and relaxation. I was astounded at how cheap Cambodia was, especially for pampering treatments such as manicures and massages. For just a few dollars I was able to relax for an hour or more while someone else looked after me. It was too good to be true and I made the most of being a "millionaire" for a few days.

In the evenings I had a wonderful routine: I ate my dinner early, then had a little ramble around the town and markets, followed by a relaxing massage treatment to finish off my day. I tried to spread my wealth and went to a different parlour each night. It's funny how I never noticed that no matter where I went I was always given a male therapist. They always said the women were busy and asked me if I would mind a male. Me being a woman of the world, I didn't care in the slightest. I was happy to let anyone massage me or paint my nails so long as I didn't have to do it myself.

One night I found out why I always had a male therapist. I asked for a full body massage, just $8 for a 90-minute massage. I couldn't believe it was that cheap, that price wouldn't even get you ten minutes in Ireland. I was shown upstairs to the treatment room, which was fine, it was all above board. There were a lot of other tourists there having massages too, so I had no need to worry.

Lying on my belly, wearing next to nothing, my massage was really good at first. My male therapist, while he was very young, had firm hands. I was surprised at how well trained he was, and his techniques were very professional. I was enjoying it immensely and felt very relaxed. He said he wanted to practise his English and asked if I would help him. I didn't mind, it was nice to chat with a local. Innocently, he asked me who I was travelling with.

Me? Travel with someone? Not a chance. I was very proud to tell him I was travelling alone and was a woman of the world. I told him confidently that I didn't need a man and had my own money. While I was banging on about being Miss Independent, without warning, he dropped his hand between my legs and asked me if I wanted "to have a good time!"

I was gobsmacked! What the hell had just happened? I wanted a massage, not optional extras, with a young boy! Where did he get that idea from? I pushed him away and scolded him. (It was hard to be angry with him as he looked about 12 years old and was trying to grow a moustache which was more like fluff under his nose.)

He said that because I was travelling alone he thought I was a sex-tourist. He even reiterated to me that for $20 I could spend the night with him. He was worried that I had misunderstood or was concerned about the price. He looked so innocent and was doing his best to look grown up and sexy. I felt really bad for him that he was selling himself so cheaply, but it wasn't the time or place to have a conversation with him about self-worth.

I declined his generous, bargain basement offer and told him that I just wanted a massage, a "normal" one. He apologised and assured me that he would "behave" for the rest of my massage. However he didn't. No sooner had he resumed my treatment when his hands started to wander all over the place again. I swiftly called time on our meeting. I was more upset about not getting my full 90 minutes than being felt up, my legs really needed a firm rub down from walking around so many temples.

I didn't want to get him into trouble. After all it was just $8 to me, he was probably only being paid one or two dollars if he was lucky. While getting dressed I caught him spying on me through the curtain. The poor kid, I really did feel sorry for him, I was old enough to be his mother and he was getting a cheap thrill from seeing my middle-aged body. I gave him a $2 dollar tip which hopefully kept him off the streets that night. There was no need to make a fuss, I knew he was just trying to earn a living. I was surprised though by what had happened. I had been all over the world on my own and it honestly never occurred to me that I would be mistaken as a sex-tourist. I am normally watching out for being ripped off or getting robbed. That was a new one even on me.

The next night I wasn't deterred by my "sexual assault" but just to be on the safe side I opted for an "above board" foot massage in a different place. For that I made sure that I was seated downstairs near the main door where it was busy. There would be no roaming hands, all I had to worry about was getting a therapist who had a foot fetish.

Sure enough I was given a male therapist, once again all the ladies were busy which was no big surprise. I was on my guard and was ready to slap him if he tried anything on with me. After just a few minutes into my massage he asked me who I was travelling with. It was like déjà vu except on this occasion, I had come prepared and was not going to get myself into trouble. I politely and loudly answered "I'm here with my husband. He is over the road having a beer and will be here soon to collect me."

It worked. My therapist never spoke to me again for the rest of the treatment. I got to relax and really enjoyed my much-needed foot massage. I had learnt my lesson. While I love travelling solo and am very proud to be a female adventure tourist, sometimes you just have to say you're with a man. Of course I shouldn't have to, but if it makes my life easier then so be it. Besides, my fictitious husband was fabulous and never let me down. He was also more than happy to take me for better or for worse and then some.

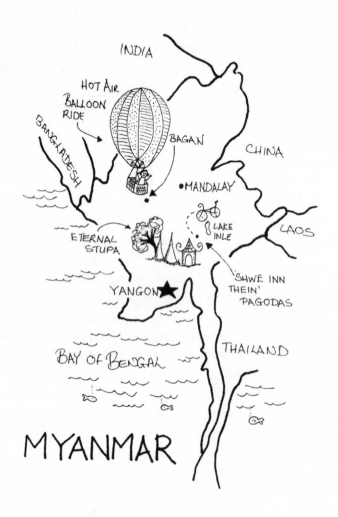

MYANMAR

Chapter 14
Golden temples, Monks & an eternal tree. Myanmar 2017

My big trip to Asia included 2 weeks in Myanmar where I was lucky enough to spend every single day out in the great outdoors, basking in glorious sunshine. It was a minimum of 30 degrees every day which was just perfect for me. I can never understand people who say it's too hot when we get 20 degrees in Ireland. I would live in a sauna if I had my way!

Myanmar was an outdoor person's dream. I spent 2 full days hiking through the centre of the country with other backpackers which brought us through remote farmlands. Our little motley crew of three Irish, one American, a German and two Czech girls followed our guide through fields and dirt tracks where we got to see authentic Burmese local life. The clock appeared to turn back in time as the locals were using such old-fashioned farming techniques. Oxen were pulling ploughs and manual labour was very much the norm. There was no intensive farming, carbon emissions or fields smothered in pesticides. It was wholesome and simple living. I loved Myanmar, it was so exceptionally tranquil and beautiful. The pace of life was slow and steady which suited my mood on the trip.

I thoroughly enjoyed the numerous boat tours I took while there. I especially loved the one which slowly sailed me down the Irrawaddy River for 12 hours on the "Road to Mandalay" (which Rudyard Kipling wrote about in his poem way back in 1890). It was very calming to relax on a deck chair and watch the world drift by.

Enthusiastically I got up in the early hours of the morning for splendid sunrises and witnessed the most amazing sunsets. I floated high above the 2,000 temples of Bagan in a bright yellow hot air balloon, gliding over the dust bowl pickled with trees and striking gold domes that reached so high I thought our basket might hit them. Unexpectedly, I made another lifelong friend while floating through the air, a lovely Indian girl, Divya. She was also travelling alone. It was her birthday and to celebrate she was treating herself to a magnificent present. As we chatted we found out we had an awful lot in common. She had also recently become single and was not sitting around crying because of it. (We high fived on that one!) After the balloon ride we went for brunch and discussed at length how lucky we were to have the gumption and tenacity to get on with life, with or without someone by our side.

I even spent a night sleeping on the floor in a Buddhist Monastery. While there, I was in a deep peaceful slumber when I was abruptly woken at 5am by an extremely loud "OM" which turned into non-stop chanting. Wearily, I peeked through the curtain to see rows and rows of bald monks, from age 5 to 105, kneeling on the hard floor in rich red robes reciting their prayers through song.

I strolled across the longest teak bridge in the world and witnessed another glorious, deep orange sunset from there. I also got eaten by mosquitoes which is obligatory when you're as sweet as me! Each and every night I searched my room and bed for tarantulas that might be hiding out there. They are native to Myanmar; I most definitely did not want to wake up beside one or accidentally bring one home in my luggage.

I was shocked and surprised by one unexpected sight while there. I never in a million years expected so much gold in Myanmar, dazzling the skyline everywhere I went. I visited numerous opulent temples, especially in Yangon the capital, which housed

140

large Buddhas adorned in bright yellow gold. They were so dazzling that I needed to wear my sunglasses even in the dark. Every corner I turned there was more gold and I wondered how it was possible that there was any gold left in the rest of the world.

As well as trekking through the countryside and sailing on boats, I tried to cycle as much as possible on my trip. I felt it would be rude not to, given how idyllic the weather was and how good I was feeling both inside and out. After my two-day trek I rented a bike. My goal was to cycle from the busy town of Inle, along the west bank of Lake Inle to Indein, where the Shwe Inn Dein Pagoda stands in all its glory. It was going to be a very pleasant and flat 65-kilometer round trip. However it would be on a robust and heavy commuter bike with a basket on the front. It was not that big a deal for me; I had all day to get there and back and was more than happy to cycle the route at a very leisurely pace. I had heard from other tourists that the Shwe Inn Dein Pagoda was an incredible place to visit and by all accounts it would certainly be worth the effort to get there. (It is a huge pagoda, dating from 12th or 13th century, which is surrounded by hundreds of little commemorative monuments (stupas) which are used to house relics or as a place of burial.)

The entire group that had been on the 2-day trek with me were also hanging around the town of Inle for a few days, and I was glad of the company. We had really bonded on the trek thanks to numerous belly laughs along the way. One of the Irish men, Colin, from my hike was joining me for the day trip. He was a really nice guy, very gentle but quietly ambitious. He told me that he hadn't ridden a bike in some time, never mind completed 65 kilometres, but he was up for an adventure and willing to try. That was good enough for me. Besides, we didn't need to go fast, we were not on Le Tour de France or its Burmese equivalent.

Funnily enough, both myself and Colin were at little crossroads in our lives. We had chatted about our respective situations on the trek and were pleasantly surprised that we had more in common than just our nationality. During the trek we bounced ideas off each other and chatted openly about love and loss which had been a key factor in both our lives. It was refreshing to hear a guy chat so openly about his hopes and dreams, as well as his pain and sorrow.

The cycle "tour" was different though because we were there to have a fun day out while enjoying the sights and sounds of the countryside. We left all our serious conversations behind us for the day, popped our bags in the baskets on our bikes and hit the open road. We both enjoyed cycling along the side of the lake, even when we occasionally hit large potholes which made us yelp at first and then laugh out loud. Sometimes we chatted endlessly, other times we cycled in silence while enjoying the journey. We had fun taking selfies and stopped a few times too for much-needed saddle breaks and cold drinks.

The wide road was not that busy thanks to "carpooling" being taken to extremes in Asia. Entire families were piled onto one little motorbike. I don't know how they kept their balance, as they made it look so effortless and comfortable. When they whizzed past us, they gave us a friendly beep, waved and smiled profusely at us. I loved the Burmese people for being so very welcoming.

Some motorbikes were used as articulated haulage trucks with piles of live produce in crates precariously stacked up behind the driver. A trail of feathers and an echo of quacking were left behind as they zipped past us. Weight was no issue for those little motorbikes, which seemed to be indestructible and capable of moving an entire village in one run. The Burmese people just got on with it, their way of life and "can do attitude" worked very efficiently. While I am not saying safety standards should be ignored, I just love that Asia is more relaxed than the Western way of life where we are bound by rules and regulations.

After a hot and dusty cycle, we arrived at our destination town of Indein. The little town was quaint as well as representing an authentic way of life. No one bothered to notice us, they were just getting on with their daily lives. Either side of the road was lined with restaurants and shop stalls. Most establishments walls were built from large cement blocks painted in bright colours, topped off with corrugated tin roofs and wide-open fronts. It was rough and ready by western standards, but I loved every bit of it. There was no need for doors, or locks for that matter. There was a great sense of freedom in Asia in comparison to our way of life with everything under lock and key. Lots of places had "outdoor dining" which in reality were red plastic tables and stools placed on the non-existent kerb which was actually the road! Locals were slurping big bowls of noodles with chopsticks, while some older gentlemen were sitting in the shade playing dominos.

After a quick food stop (more rice for me,) we set about visiting the beautiful temple. A highly polished marble stairway welcomed us and led us up to the main temple. At the top of the stairs there was a large Buddha in a whitewashed shrine. The entire complex was a large cemetery, yet to me, it felt so much more spiritual and heavenly than the ones we have in Ireland. Maybe it was the contrast of the blue sky and endless gold trimmings that made it look so vibrant and Godly to me. Perhaps it was the little bells that were chiming gently in the breeze along with hundreds of pungent incense sticks burning that added to the tranquil atmosphere for those resting in peace. Either way, I felt a very deep sense of calm and inner peace while there.

We wandered around the complex and saw the many varieties of stupas. They all looked like inverted ice cream cones; each one had a fat base which tapered upwards into a point. Some had been restored and looked truly magnificent. They were in excellent condition, covered in gold and reaching high into the air, aiming for the heavens. In contrast, the older ones that were hundreds of years old were crumbling away as they were made of mud or oak. In my opinion, even though they were disintegrating, time had been kinder to the older ones as some of them had trees growing precariously out of them. A small shoot must have taken hold inside the stupa and over time proceeded to grow lopsided through the cracks, towards the sun. I imagined their roots were gently hugging the stupa and the remains inside. Even though those stupas were badly "damaged" I loved them the most. I decided there and then that when I die, I want a tree to grow "out" of me. I think it would be like having eternal life while being one with nature at the same time.

Further on we went up more stairs where we came upon the VIP cemetery. There were hundreds of tightly packed stupas which were bigger than me. Some were completely covered, head to toe, in gold. I was unbelievably tempted to try and peel some of the gold splendour off them. I knew it was just gold-leaf paint as opposed to solid gold, but still, there was a little devil inside me that just wanted to put an end to my curiosity. I managed to resist my urge, but I can tell you it wasn't easy.

The cycle around the lake to get here had been more than worth the effort. The Shwe Inn Dein Pagoda with its mish mash of stupas looked amazing in the tourist books but in reality was simply outstanding. I was very glad we had cycled our heavy bikes around the lake to get there. There was just one problem: we never considered the effort required to cycle back.

The return cycle was a little taxing to be honest, even for a seasoned cyclist like me. We were both tired from the heat and sightseeing. Had we been smart about it we should have taken a water taxi back to our town and paid a little extra for the bikes. The great thing about Asia is that you can pay for just about anything to get done. The locals would have been more than willing to earn a little more, except we didn't think of that!

Between the distance and the weight of our bikes we both struggled badly on the way back. Slowly, slowly we cycled northwards beside Lake Inle along with a continuous stream of motorbikes and trucks. We just kept going; we were so tired we couldn't even chat to each other but nonetheless we stuck side by side for moral support. The sun began to set on our long day, and eventually, much to our relief, our town's lights became visible across the bridge. Myself and Colin had had a perfect day even if it was a little more physically demanding than we anticipated.

Even though cycling in Myanmar was not as challenging as other mammoth days out on my bike, it is such a lovely memory to have. I was especially glad of the company for the day. While we were both wrecked we made time for another big bowl of noodles to finish off our adventure. We chuckled about the saddle sores we had for souvenirs, but overall, we agreed that it had been a brilliant day out.

What I remember most from my journey to Myanmar is its colours. The cloudless sky was cornflower blue. Dazzling gold reflected off the bright yellow sun, making the country seem even brighter than it already was. There were glorious sunsets that turned the entire sky deep orange, making the dusty temples of Bagan a perfect silhouette on the skyline. I will never forget the red dusty roads and the bright yellow hot air balloon that I sailed through the sky in. Myanmar was the light that I needed to remind me that following every sunset, there is always a sunrise to look forward to.

My heartbreak was left firmly back in 2017. I was moving forward into another new phase in my life. I felt different too, I was more emotionally "together" from my trip. I had thought long and hard about myself, my boundaries and what I deserved. I would rather be single and happy forever than settle for a relationship that made me cry.

Coming home to Ireland in early January I was refreshed, brown as berry, full of sunshine and glowing from the inside out. I was "me" again and was ready to take on the world in 2018. My quality time alone and being immersed into two other cultures had done me the world of good. Winter was drawing to a close in Ireland too; the days were starting to get a little longer and brighter. Spring and new beginnings were just days away and I could see daffodils starting to poke their head out of the soil in my garden which made me smile. Even better, in just a few weeks' time I would be back cycling in the south of Spain with Cormac and another new gang of eager cyclists. As if that wasn't enough I also had 2 huge cycling trips to look forward to in 2018.

Chapter 15
Unless you faint, puke or die, keep pedalling.
Colombia 2018

While I had the time of my life in Asia travelling solo, I felt excited to go on a cycling trip in June, to France with my friends. In truth, I wanted to surround myself with others. I had readjusted to single life but that didn't mean I wanted to spend every moment of my life alone.

Four years had passed since my horrific struggle on La Marmotte and while it was never going to be forgotten, I had made my peace with the event for trying to break me. The time had come to say "bonjour" once again to France and make new memories, better ones! Five of us arrived in beautiful Provence where Mont Ventoux, one of the most famous cycling summits in the world, was waiting for us.

Thanks to some amazing engineers there were three tough routes all leading to the summit of Mont Ventoux. So like any good group of enthusiastic cyclists, we cycled up Mont Ventoux, which is nicknamed the Beast of Provence, via all three routes in one day!

While conquering the Beast three times in one day was tough, it was a wonderful challenge and gave me membership to the elite

Club des Cinglés du Mont Ventoux. Best of all the day went without a hitch, the weather was perfect and so were my legs. I was pleasantly surprised that due to my months of intensive training there were no tantrums or an ounce of pain! In fact, to this day, it is one of the most "perfect" days I have ever had on my bike. It renewed my love for France and helped me realise that I was becoming a highly accomplished cyclist. Upon our return home, my cycling club mates were super impressed by my achievement. Honestly, I hadn't realised how fit and strong I was, or how out of the ordinary my trips were becoming. To me, it was just a case of cycle until you get to the top, stop when you arrive, repeat twice more!

The months and years were flying by. It was hard to believe with all my amazing trips and adventures how I had once felt about myself and my life. I was truly living the dream. I was in a wonderful routine of working hard while doing what I love. I was having fun with my friends both on and off my bike. I was visiting Cormac and Spain every March for fun in the sun and had even added extra dates in October too. I had also set up weekend Yoga breaks in Ireland that were a great success. Life was plain sailing and I wanted for nothing. (Not even a husband.) Enthusiastically I rolled out of bed each day and made the most of all the time I had.

I was delighted too, that after a year of hard work and self-reflection I graduated and had a new Diploma in Life and Business Coaching. It wasn't easy going back to college and doing assignments, but I persevered anyway and qualified with flying colours.

It was a great course to do for professional reasons, but I also found it a huge help for my own personal development and emotional intelligence. It highlighted to me that I still needed a little help (a lot if I am honest) in the romance and self-worth department. Even after all the years I had put into my mental health there was still room for improvement and there were a few issues that needed fine tuning.

The diploma had forced me to take another hard look at myself, and on reflection I could see I had been making the same mistakes over and over, yet always expected a different result. I had never known my worth or valued myself enough. I always settled for less than I deserved and been miserable as a result. I knew that I had to change my patterns and beliefs if I wanted different results in the romance department in the future. There was no other way forward. I had to be brave, take responsibility for my happiness and stop making poor choices, (settling for crap!) Once again I was happy to be a work in progress and unravel where exactly I had been going wrong all my life when it came to romantic relationships. Luckily, it was December, and I had a very long flight from Frankfurt in Germany to Bogota in Colombia to think about my behaviour and have my annual appraisal with myself.

When I told people I was travelling to Colombia solo they unconsciously gave a little gasp followed by a hard swallow. I knew exactly what they were thinking. Colombia was infamous for narcotics and Pablo Escobar; how could it possibly be a safe destination for a solo woman? Even my family were more worried than usual about me travelling there alone, after all, according to my mother, I could potentially be kidnapped or used as a drug mule. It was an unfair reputation and there was no need for anyone to worry. I had done my research, plus, lots of friends I'd made through travelling had been there and loved it.

The country had everything to make it an ideal destination. There was culture, jungles and Caribbean coast lines. There was the Lost City (La Ciudad Perdida) too. Since the very first time I had read about it I wanted to go there, and it was top of my itinerary for the trip. If all that was not enough, as luck would have it, Colombia was renowned for cycling, and I planned on going for a bike ride while I was there.

Exactly one year after my trip to Myanmar I touched down in Colombia's capital, Bogota. While the altitude tested me a lot on arrival, (Bogota is a whopping 2,644 metres above sea level) it was nowhere near as bad as when I was in Bolivia or the Himalayas. The craziness of the airport did not help much either but as it was my third time in South America I was fully prepared to run the gauntlet to the Salida/Exit. South American arrivals halls are chaotic to say the least, plus there are always loads of people looking to rip off "newbie" tourists. Holding my head high I walked with confidence and made a beeline for the door. Without any hassle I immediately found the line of yellow taxis right outside the arrivals area. My conversational Spanish had improved significantly by that time too and in my best Irish-Spanish accent I instructed my friendly driver where we were going. Even though I was very tired, I couldn't wait to explore as much of Colombia as I could in 25 days.

For my first full day I joined a free cycling tour of Bogota. There was no way I was going to miss that. I really needed to get outdoors after the extremely long flight. I also wanted to stretch my legs and get my pasty winter skin out in the sun. It felt so good to be in the heat on a bike and enjoy the brightness of the sun. Bogota was huge but the bike tour was mainly through the old town where most of the culture and beautiful old buildings were. It felt so nice to potter around slowly on a bike while learning all about Colombia's past, present and future. (Please note, there is so much more to Colombia than drug lords!)

While the city bike tour showed me all the important buildings in Bogota it was really a warm-up for greater things that were yet to come. Colombia is famous for the number of professional cyclists it has produced over the years and more noteworthy are the tough, relentless mountains in the Andes which those professionals train on. My cycling goal for my time in Colombia was to cycle the longest climb on earth, the Alto de Letras. Obviously it was not going to be the easiest route on the planet, but I was feeling very positive about attempting it. I was happy that I was in super shape thanks to my three trips to the top of Mont Ventoux, as well as hours and hours of hard-core training prior to departure.

Before I took on my mammoth cycle I had lots of time to explore Colombia. I flew from Bogota to the north coast and arrived in the Caribbean city of Santa Marta. From there I joined a trekking tour with nineteen others. Finally, I was going to tick a box off my bucket list and visit the Lost City, "La Ciudad Perdida." (It is deep in the jungle and was once home to 8000 people. The Lost City is now an archaeological site which was looted of all its treasures upon discovery in 1972.)

The Lost City was hidden deep in a dense jungle which took us two full days to walk into and another two days to get back out of. On the plus side that meant there were no hordes of tourists in coaches to contend with or souvenir shops selling tat. Myself and my adventurous group had an absolutely great time on the route. Those few days were definitely a huge, memorable highlight in my life. The entire 4 days were so much better than I ever expected. Much to my surprise, the sleeping conditions weren't rough at all. There were purpose-built camps with bunk beds, outdoor kitchens and "proper" toilets along the jungle trail. They were not glamorous by any means but a hundred times better than the tent and creepy crawlies I had expected!

When I trekked through the jungle and came to a viewing point, it was only then that I could truly appreciate the expanse and lushness of Colombia. I especially enjoyed being far away from civilisation and out in nature. It was wonderful to be "unplugged" from life and having time to recharge my own battery instead of my phones. All I had to do was carry my little rucksack, follow the guide and have fun bathing in the river each night. I enjoyed being part of a group too. We were all so different, not just our nationalities but our lives, yet we all had the same goal and common interest. I made some great friends along the way, most notably Monika from Madrid. We were like two peas in a pod. She was traveling solo too and had lots of funny stories from her many worldwide adventures. I loved having another solo female on the trip; we chatted endlessly about life, travel, romance, celebrity gossip and all the other hot topics that two modern, single women feel are important. We both had similar itineraries too and planned to meet each other later on in our travels.

The trip to and from the Lost City did have its moments. I never expected to see soldiers in full combat gear, deep in the jungle on our trail, toting humongous machine guns, handguns and grenades! There used to be a big problem with tourists getting kidnapped along the route but funnily enough, it's not such a problem anymore, thanks to the military presence.

From trekking deep in the jungle I headed west to the gorgeous colonial city of Cartagena which was extremely busy due to the festive season. I loved walking around the old town and enjoyed a boat trip to the idyllic Rosario Islands. It turned out that Colombia was a great way to enjoy the Caribbean on a budget. The island I went to was better than any photos I had seen of 5-star destinations in Barbados. There was pure white sand that was soft and delicate under my feet. The sea was crystal clear; at times it looked blue before it changed to a light turquoise with silver strands. I lay for hours on a sun lounger under lush palm trees where I relaxed my tired body and recovered from my jungle expedition.

On Christmas eve I made a fatal mistake. Monika and I met up once again in Cartagena. We spent a glorious day relaxing on the beach having fun, chatting and splashing in the sea. At the end of the day we went to a small restaurant and ate some freshwater prawns. They were cooked but just not enough. I knew the minute I had eaten them that I was in serious trouble. Sure enough I was right. After two hours I was violently projectile vomiting. Within three hours the most horrific diarrhoea started. I was drenched in sweat, turned green and could not keep anything down, not even water. I was floored. I had never ever been so sick in all my life. I was only halfway through my trip of a lifetime and didn't know if I could continue. I kept hoping it was just a "24-hour thing" and with some rest it would pass. Monika was kind enough to go to the pharmacy for me, but nothing was working.

I could hardly leave my hotel room let alone think of travelling any further. I was due to meet my cycling guide in two days' time. He was just a short internal flight away, but it might as well have been on another planet. I was very upset, tired and hungry. I had gone all that way, trained hard and was determined to cycle the longest climb on earth.

I did my best to enjoy Christmas day in Cartagena. I had a day trip booked which would take me in a small boat down the mangroves which wasn't exactly easy as I was so sick. The next day, the time came to say goodbye to my new friend and nurse. I was so glad that I had Monika there to help me. It's never nice to be alone and sick. She was really good to me, and I am eternally grateful to her.

In preparation for my short flight I ate and drank absolutely nothing, I figured it would be better to be safe than sorry. Thankfully my starvation tactic worked, and I managed to fly to the large city of Medellin without any accidents. (Medellin was once the hometown of the notorious drug lord Pablo Escobar.)

Even though there was no let up with my food poisoning, I managed to sightsee a little and enjoy my time in Medellin. The only way I could get through each day was by eating copious amounts of Imodium and drinking litres of Pepto Bismol. Neither was working very well but combined they bought me a little time to leave my hostel and explore the city. I took a walking tour through Comuna 13. The "suburb" was high up on the side of the valley wall, right beside the jungle and overlooking downtown Medellin. It was from this neighbourhood the drug lords used to run their lucrative "business." Logistically it was perfect for them to smuggle their narcotics deep into the dense jungle and onwards for global export. The Comuna was interesting to say the least; thankfully it is no longer a drug den but a thriving area thanks to tourism.

While relaxing over lunch I checked my emails. I still had not heard from my cycling guide and was beginning to get rather concerned. I had emailed him the previous day just to touch base and confirm I was on my way. However, there was no reply. I had also paid him in advance some time ago for three nights' accommodation and two full days of guided cycling and bike hire, so as you can imagine I was beginning to wonder if I had been duped.

He eventually contacted me and changed all our meeting arrangements on a whim. I was so annoyed as there was a "drug lord tour" I would have gone on, but it clashed with our previous meeting time. I was pissed off to say the least, because I had wanted to learn all about how Colombia overcame the Narcos.

I should have guessed that my guide was not exactly interested in working that week. It was just after Christmas, and it turned out he had some friends from America visiting him on the same days that he was supposed to be working with me. From the very outset he had been vague with the itinerary, kept getting my nationality wrong, mixing up my name with someone else and then to top it all off, when we eventually met he had the cheek to tell me I was "difficult to deal with"! Now I do not know about you, but when I pay for a guided trip, a lot of money by the way, I expect to be treated like a priority.

His business partner threatened to cancel my tour when I expressed my frustration at their lack of customer service. As much as it pained me, I ended up apologising to them so that my tour could go ahead. It was the only thing I could do since I needed them for the cycling excursion and logistics. I didn't want to cycle around Colombia on my own, besides, for a start, I had no idea where the longest climb in the world was.

As if meeting them wasn't stressful enough, my food poisoning was getting progressively worse. I was completely drained of every bodily fluid imaginable. I was losing weight with each passing hour. I was tired, irritable, emotional and totally dehydrated. I could hardly stand up straight for severe cramps and in general, I was in a complete heap. I was guzzling anti-sickness tablets to try and bind me up. I also had to consume litres of electrolytes to keep myself hydrated and worst of all, I desperately tried not to pass wind as I couldn't be guaranteed what the outcome might be. I was so deflated and upset. It felt as if someone, perhaps the universe, or "God" were all trying to tell me to quit cycling.

Five days had passed since I had eaten an actual meal and I was emaciated. My clothes were swinging loosely around my waist, and my face was so hollow that my teeth looked too big for my mouth. I was grey in colour and my eyes had sunk deep into the back of my head. While I was delighted to be lighter both for my bikini and for cycling up hills, I had zero energy and was just about hanging on to life. I wondered if I would just keel over and die. Indeed, the way I felt I wouldn't have minded if I did. I wished I could turn back the clock and not have eaten the prawns but as we all know, the clock only goes forward and there are times in life when you just have to accept what has happened.

As for the guide, truth be told, I would definitely turn the clock back and never have booked him! I had thoroughly researched cycling tour companies in Colombia and had chosen his company over many other businesses. They seemed to be the most professional by a long shot according to their glowing reviews online. (That's a bit of a worry in itself!) However, to be fair, his business partner was lovely. He was definitely the business brains, and it showed. I'm sure if he had dealt with my initial emails and booking from the outset, things would have gone very differently. He was very organised, attentive and kind towards me. He went to the pharmacy and got me litres of electrolyte drinks and other medications. He also checked in on me regularly which made me feel cared for.

Their friends who were tagging along on the trip, (though in fact I was really tagging along with them), were pleasant enough and did chat in English to me. I did feel like a spare wheel (excuse the pun) as I was the only paying guest on the "tour" but with me feeling so sick, I didn't have the energy to care what the group dynamics were like.

The night before the big challenge we stayed in a lovely town called Honda. It was a beautiful colonial town with many bridges over the Magdalena River. In its heyday it was an important market town and even boasts the first iron bridge built in South America. Unfortunately I didn't get to see as much of the town as I would have liked as I was desperately trying to get solid food to stay in my tummy.

I managed to eat a plain burger which was sitting pretty well in my gut. I was feeling hopeful that my food poisoning had run its course and that I was on the mend. However, with an impending 80-kilometre gruelling uphill, with 3,675 metres of climbing (that is a serious climb), I was going to need a lot more fuel than that. Even if I was in the best of health, the longest climb on earth was a big ask for my body. I had a feeling I was in for a hellish day on my bike, I just didn't know on a scale of 1-10 how bad it would be.

My guide took a lot of time to explain in great detail all the important points of the route to me. I was a bit confused as to why he was going into so much detail; after all I had paid him to ride beside me for the day, surely he could tell me as we cycled along the route? He showed me Ruta National 50 on the map which links Manizales and San Sebastian de Mariquita and explained that the route has featured many times on the Vuelta a Colombia (Pro tour of Colombia.) There were 3 notable towns along the route. I was to expect them at 20, 40 and 60km, which was easy to remember. After the third town the route would get even harder. I had to prepare myself for a very tough 14 kilometres due to it being very steep. That part of the route would take me above 3000m altitude, and I would be practically up in the clouds! He assured me that my breathing in the thin air wouldn't be a problem. I would be gaining altitude gradually throughout the day so that I would naturally acclimatize along the way. I tried to reassure myself that I had just recently been to France and was used to tough climbs, and this would be no different. Nevertheless, doubt screamed loudly in my head and reminded me that I would already have cycled uphill continuously for 60 kilometres before that section. I wondered what the hell was I thinking when I booked the cycling trip? I was seriously regretting it. I tried to nod and smile as he prattled on and on with the logistics. I was feeling weak as it was and just didn't have the capacity for any of his instructions.

There was some good news, he told me. After 74 kilometres I would get my first respite, because there would be a rewarding flat section and then just a short drag to the finish. It sounded horrendous, all of it, even the flat bit. My head was spinning, and I was beginning to wonder if I should just cut my losses and not bother. I questioned myself, my sanity especially. Part of me kept saying that I didn't need to make my life so hard. No one would care if I did the route or not. In fact most people had no idea it existed so what difference would it make if I quit before I started? My tummy gave a nice big gurgle to remind me that the cycle was not the only challenge ahead.

I lay awake most of the night deciding what to do. On the one hand I couldn't bear to think that I had paid the guide in advance and potentially he would not have to do anything for it. That was galling me the most. There was no way I wanted to let him off the hook and to make good money out of me for nothing. On the other hand there was a real possibility that I might die of exhaustion on the way up the road!

Stubbornness got the better of me. There was no way I was quitting without a fight. I decided to at least try to cycle some of the route. If I needed to, I could get in the van and call it quits at any time. I was happy with my decision and felt it was a good compromise to my dilemma.

I was dressed in my cycling kit and ready for action at 7am. I popped my Snoopy teddy in my back pocket: I knew I was going to need to call on him for moral support during the day. Once again I pumped my body with more medication and tried to eat some dry toast. On the bright side the morning was stunning, there was not one cloud in the sky, and it was a very comfortable temperature in the mid-twenties. The official start point in San Sebastian de Mariquita was just 495 metres above sea level. Throughout the day I would cycle through numerous climate zones before finally finishing in the highlands at some 3800 metres above sea level. I could look forward to extremely high humidity which lets the dense vegetation grow abundantly.

One of the "tagging along" friends and I were driven close to the base of the climb to make the day a little easier for us. The other two cyclists, my guide and his other buddy, cycled all the way from the hotel to the start. The plan was the stronger cyclists would easily catch up with us. They sure did. Not only did they catch us, but they proceeded to cycle straight past us and kept going at a very fast pace. What the heck?

I was the paying guest and my guide had just left me. All I saw was the back of him! It was no wonder he went through the route with me in such detail. He clearly never had any intention of cycling with me from the outset. So much for paying him a lot of money to guide me. As he cycled past me he said hello or something of the sort. I wasn't so polite. Colombia is a huge country, around the same size as South Africa, so just to be sure he heard me I shouted obscenities at him as loudly as I could. Oh well. I didn't like him much from the very outset and he probably would have annoyed me for the day anyway. Perhaps I was better off on my own. I still thought he was an idiot though. He ditched his only paying client to hang out with his friend and show off.

The chap that started out with me pushed on ahead too as he was much faster than me. I didn't mind that at all, after all I hadn't paid him to stay with me. There was no way I could go any faster or try to keep up with him. I was too worried about the length of the route to burn all my matches early on. Otherwise, I actually felt all right. I was happy enough in myself and my ability. I wondered if I was miraculously cured of my food poisoning but then perhaps, that was wishful thinking as I was only 30 minutes and 5 kilometres into the cycle.

Mentally I was prepared for the challenge and was more than confident that I could do it even if it took me all day. When I booked the trip I never once doubted my physical ability. Even if I ran out of motivation I could most certainly rely on my stubborn streak to get me over the finish line. Yet I was never prepared for feeling so awful. After just one hour of cycling a niggle of a defeatist attitude arrived in my head. I was worried. While I have suffered physical pain during events in the past this was a whole new emotional level for me. I didn't like it one bit. I knew I was tired and emotional which was not helping matters. I was emaciated and malnourished too which never makes for "sane" thinking. I certainly did not want to entertain the thoughts that found their way into my psyche but what was I supposed to do with them? I was all alone on my bike in the middle of nowhere and I had no one to talk to. I was lonely, it was just me, my crazy thoughts and miles of open road ahead of me. How the heck would I overcome those feelings of failure and keep going?

I wanted to stop and cry but I knew if I put my foot to the ground that would be the end of me. I had to keep going no matter how slowly. My legs were like jelly and would not move the pedals with any gusto. I was pretty sure I would be faster walking. Trying to keep my mind off my pain and anguish I really did try as best as I could to enjoy the experience, I was in Colombia on a trip of a lifetime after all.

Along the route I cycled passed three big black vultures which were sitting on a wall. In my mind they were like cartoon characters who were eyeing me up as prey. I desperately hoped they weren't hungry as I was an easy target. When they didn't budge a muscle I was sure they were having a good laugh at my expense. I could practically hear them mocking me and deciding that I was too skinny and pathetic looking to eat. They agreed they would wait for something meatier to come past and have a substantial meal instead.

After four long hours my back started to scream, the balls of my feet were burning and to add to my misery I got saddle sores and chafing. It would seem that on this trip, food poisoning alone wasn't enough. What little motivation I had at the start of the day was long gone. It was probably with my very expensive guide who was still nowhere to be seen. To pass the time I pretended he was cycling beside me. I kept swearing out loud at him and telling him exactly what I thought of his customer service or rather lack of it. It made me laugh and momentarily I stopped feeling sorry for myself. I busied myself inventing new obscenities and phrases which helped to pass the time and a few metres. However, even though I never stopped cycling, the kilometres were still not passing quickly enough. I was stuck on that God-forsaken climb, and I really was hating every minute of it. Had the van been anywhere to be seen I probably would have climbed into it. Maybe it was a good thing that I was left to my own devices. Otherwise quitting would have been too easy.

Through thick and thin over the years I had always managed to pull a little secret stash of gumption out of my soul and overcome my difficulties. On that route, I was sure that I was going to snap, physically and mentally. Would the Alto de Letras be the one to break me? Well, it sure was doing its best!

Even passing through the towns and seeing other humans didn't help me much. The locals didn't bother to notice me as I struggled through their metropolis. Everyone was busy with their own lives and rightly so. The three towns my guide had mentioned eventually came and went. I passed the 60-kilometre mark and that was the end of civilisation for the day. On the plus side the temperature was very pleasant up in the mountains which I was grateful for. My guide was right about one thing: the altitude wasn't a problem at all. I never noticed the air becoming thinner or felt that my breathing was becoming laboured. I checked in with myself every so often by shouting obscenities just to be sure I was not dying.

After six hours I had to change tactics and began having full blown conversations with my Snoopy teddy. When our conversation ran dry I sang songs to myself. Not knowing the words didn't matter in the slightest. I just improvised with more swearing. I was beginning to wonder if I had got Tourette's Syndrome as well as food poisoning!

On the bright side my computer finally showed some progress. I had completed just over 65 kilometres and had the back of the 80 kilometres broken. Finally I could actually think about finishing at some stage in the day.

While my guide had chosen not to cycle with his paying guest that day his business partner was providing a support vehicle for all of us. Dividing his time between the "groups" sporadically he came to my aid. However for the last two hours of my journey I had him all to myself. Everyone else had finished the climb and were patiently (or impatiently) waiting at the top for me. He drove behind me at times, sometimes he went on ahead and handed me food as I went past. I loved having him all to myself. I did feel bad that I was going so slow and taking so long to complete the route but what could I do? The others hadn't got food poisoning and lost half their body weight. As well as that, one of them had my guide cycling beside him for the day. They would just have to wait for me: it's not like I could go any faster, or slower for that matter.

With approximately one hour left of cycling time before I finished, out of nowhere my guide magically appeared before me. At first I thought it was some sort of an apparition, but it wasn't. He was very real. My guide dollied up beside me on his bike, looking fresh and happy. In comparison I was absolutely hanging on by a thread. Without thinking, he decided I needed to hear his advice on how to cycle. He began telling me what to do and how to stretch. He even told me that I would be better off trying to cycle in a straight line instead of wobbling all over the place.

Now I will admit to being very tired and emotional at that time. I was at 3,300 metres above sea level with around 8 kilometres left to complete. I was not in any sort of humour to hear his stupid remarks. Contrary to what he thought, I was doing my best to cycle in a straight line. In fact, I was somewhat busy just trying to stay upright and alive. Gosh it was painful having him there. He was just being ridiculous and a complete pain in the saddle. Whilst cycling beside me he decided I needed a demonstration. Like a peacock he fluffed up his feathers, jumped up out of his saddle and started stretching. He was wiggling his backside around whilst simultaneously telling me to look at him.

I LOST IT!

The goddam cheek of that man. I had got myself that far (72 km) and really did not appreciate his inane comments. I politely, with the help of my new obscenities, asked him to go away and leave me alone. I assured him I was having "fun" on my own. The audacity of him really annoyed me. I was dying. My body was in bits and my mental health was somewhere miles back on the road. To top it off that twit was giving me instructions after ignoring me for the entire day. Refund please!

Thankfully he left with his tail between his legs, but his lovely business partner stayed close by. He took a few photos of me and kept my water bottles topped up. As I was so close to the top, motorists that passed by me beeped and cheered me on as they whizzed by. I really appreciated their support and desperately tried to smile and wave back at them. My pedals turned just that little bit faster with every passing car. Those well-wishers managed to revive my broken spirit. I could even hear my Snoopy teddy shouting from my back pocket cheering me on. From the depths of my soul my single-minded resolve was slowly being reignited. I knew that I could make it to the top. I had just three more kilometres to drag myself through. All I had to do was keep going and soon it would all be over!

Eventually, in the distance I could see the van parked up and waiting for my big arrival. At first I thought it was a mirage but how could it be? My bike computer had moved all the way from zero kilometres to just under eighty. I was in the last few hundred metres. Wearily looking up, through my hazy eyes I was able to make out the group standing beside the vehicle. They were waving profusely, and I could hear faint cheers. I desperately tried my best to sit upright on my bike and attempted to look lively. I was magnetised by the van and pretended it was sucking me into its force field; it was getting bigger and bigger the closer it came. My legs somehow managed to turn a little faster and I started to feel human again. Even though I was in excruciating pain, I was filled with pride and excitement. I had just a few metres to go. The cheers got louder, and my legs pushed one final pedal stroke. My bike and I freewheeled into the middle of the group. I planted my feet on the soil at the top of the Alto de Letras. I was 3,679 meters above sea level.

I touched the van to make sure it was real. I had completed the longest climb on earth, probably in the longest time too but who cares?

I had done it, even though the odds were hugely stacked against me. I was proud that I never gave up. My Giant Tortoise tactics from France must have secretly been egging me on the whole time. I was floored and honestly, I felt like I needed to puke from exhaustion but there was nothing left inside me. I managed to smile for some photos and then wobbled my way into the van. I was never so glad in all my life to sit down and be still.

From the summit we drove to a beautiful town called Manizales and spent the night in a hotel before going our separate ways. Needless to say there wasn't exactly a send-off for me. Nor was I asked to fill out a customer feedback form! I was sorry that my guide had not worked out for me as I expected. I would have loved to have learnt about Colombia from a local and I most definitely could have used some company on the climb. However, what was done was done. I was just glad that I had survived the cycle.

Unfortunately the stress of the cycle caused my body even more trauma and I became extremely ill, much worse than I already was. In hindsight there is no way I should have cycled while sick and it probably was one of the most stupid things I have ever done but at the same time, I would have regretted it if I hadn't. New Year's Eve was a total washout. I spent it in bed watching Disney movies in Spanish between snoozes. I am sure my body was in shock and just needed time out. After two days' bed rest, for my last excursion of the trip I visited a very upmarket coffee plantation, Hacienda Venecia. I learnt a lot about Colombian coffee in between periodically running to the loo. I even picked coffee berries off the trees too. When I burst them open I was thrilled to find my very own, perfectly formed little coffee bean inside each one.

While I was sad to leave Colombia, I couldn't wait to get home. I had lost even more weight and was practically living on fresh air. Getting back to Ireland was a major struggle though. I did my absolute best with a cocktail of drugs and electrolytes. I stopped eating 24 hours before my long-haul flight to Europe and didn't dare take as much as a sip of water while onboard. It was all I could do to ensure I didn't have any embarrassing accidents on my very long flight from Bogota to Frankfurt and onwards to Dublin.

By the time I returned to Ireland I had a full-blown gastro infection. I crawled into Accident and Emergency in a Dublin hospital. I was green, vomiting, shaking, sweating and weak as a kitten. To be honest if I had died right there and then on the floor I wouldn't have cared. In fact it would have been a very pleasant relief.

Thankfully that's not what happened. The medical team kept me alive by pumping me full of antibiotics. I had picked up Shigella, a rod-shaped bacterium from contaminated food or water. I knew it was that damn prawn. Luckily, though, I was home and safe. I was very happy to spend four days relaxing in hospital, (at least, it was nice once the shivers and vomiting stopped). Not only was my stomach glad of the medical team but my legs were especially happy to rest and recover from the cycle. After what I had been through I wholeheartedly enjoyed lying motionless in my hospital bed watching rubbish daytime TV through very blurry eyes. I bet I was the easiest patient they ever had.

Every cloud has a silver lining. On the plus side I had a great tan and didn't have to worry about January blubber. I also found out much to my surprise who my friends were. It's funny, some people that I considered to be close friends didn't pick up the phone, let alone visit me in hospital. Yet two people whom I considered to be mere acquaintances came barrelling in the door laden down with gifts and smiles. It was an eye-opener to say the least, and one that didn't go unnoticed. At first I made excuses for my friends' behaviour. They were possibly extremely busy or perhaps they had not read my messages. However, even that was hard to justify to myself after sitting in hospital for four full days. I asked myself if I was expecting too much of my friends, was I being too demanding or needy? I had often been told over the years that I was "too much for people" and once upon a time I was warned that "not everyone thinks like you."

I had taken those insights very much to heart. I know that I am overly enthusiastic. I like to connect regularly with friends and make plans to meet up. I guess my overly zealous actions scare people off, as I have had many calls go unanswered, not returned for weeks and in some cases, I never heard from the person ever again. Sitting in the hospital just reminded me that while I have many faults, neglecting to reach out to others is not one of them.

On reflection, I didn't think a phone call was asking too much of my close friends. In the age of technology it is easy to call, text, send videos and be "virtually" there for those that matter to you. Perhaps they didn't know what to say or maybe they didn't want to hear about my illness but either way, I felt very let down. I knew that I would never treat a friend that way and while I could appreciate that not everyone thinks like I do, it was a hard pill to swallow.

I learned a very valuable lesson that week. Moving forward, I needed to make sure my friendships were genuine and that we both contributed to the relationship. In time, in fact quite naturally, some "friends" drifted away. I was very grateful for those who did show up for me when the chips were down, and I made sure from then on to nurture those connections.

Chapter 16
Dolo-mighty
Italy 2019

While I was technically better when I got out of hospital,
I had to take it easy for a while. Not only had my gut
health taken a beating, but I was stick-thin. My body
was craving so much rest that for once in my life I was more than
happy to listen to it. I also was very much enjoying letting those that
did care about me, look after me. It was a welcome change to be
vulnerable for once. Sometimes I'm so busy being me that I forget
to show the world that while I am resilient, I am human too.

Due to my food poisoning I hadn't managed to reflect on my
personal development as much as I had wanted to while in Colombia and on my long flight home. I really noticed that I missed not
having checked in with myself and felt a little "nude" without it. My
annual appraisal was a ritual with myself that I loved and no matter
how well I was doing in life, I enjoyed checking in on my progress
and keeping myself on track. I was even more enthusiastic about
my appraisal since I had completed my life coaching course. Not
only was I officially qualified to help other people move their life
forwards for the better, but I could also sort out my own crap in a

more professional and structured capacity. I was the perfect client to practise my new skills on. I felt strongly that if I couldn't help myself, then how could I expect to help others?

In January, I took that time to think about my life, about what I wanted to achieve personally and professionally while creating lots of exciting new goals. 2019 might have been the year of the pig in the Chinese calendar, but for me, I earmarked it as the year of pleasure! Top of my list was to have fun and lots of it. My "near death" experience had been a very good reminder that I was pushing myself too hard and that my life was once again out of balance. I could not live on adrenaline alone; it was not healthy physically or mentally. Sooner or later something was bound to give. In reflection the prawn was just "the straw that broke the camel's back" so to speak. It was a little poke from someone "above" reminding me that I am not invincible.

The time had come for me to stop and smell the roses, slow down and be a human being rather than a human doing. I made sure that 2019 was unbelievably fantastic in every possible way. I ran riot with my passport, touching down in Iceland, Finland, Estonia, Italy, Spain, Portugal and Cuba. I spent time in historical buildings, relaxed in coffee shops while watching the world go by. I ate weird and wonderful foods that were local delicacies (no prawns) and took walking tours to learn about the cities I was visiting. Closer to home I had numerous weekends away in Ireland and made sure I only went to hotels with spa facilities. I got lots of massages and relaxed in Jacuzzis whenever possible.

I was quite the social butterfly that year too. I frequented restaurants and parties at weekends, went out with friends at every given opportunity and never once rejected any invitations that came my way. There was an abundance of fun as well as so much laughter. My social diary was so busy that at times it felt like work was getting in the way of my hectic schedule.

However, as much as I needed to have a "down year" on my bike I already had a trip to Italy booked with my cycling friends. I thought about cancelling it but decided what the heck! I didn't have to cycle every day if I didn't want to. After all there are plenty of other things to do besides killing yourself on a bike. (Eating pizza and gelato to name a few!)

We went to the Dolomites in north-east Italy, practically in Austria, and to this day it is one of the most beautiful places I have ever been to on earth. While the area is famous for cycling it is also notorious for big steep climbs. Most of the routes we planned to cycle have been featured in the Giro d'Italia professional tour.

Every morning, from my bedroom window, I looked in amazement at the backdrop to our town. It was set in the foothill of the Dolomites Mountain range. They were unique, not just for their dolomitic limestone; it was their jagged imposing shape that sets them apart from all the other mountains in the world. They looked like a row of serrated knives reaching high into the sky. It's no wonder they received UNESCO World Heritage status.

While the Dolomites are a cyclist's paradise there was one major problem: the heat! Europe was being scorched alive that year with daily averages of 37 degrees in Corvara, our chosen destination town. We got up early to get going on our bikes but even then it was impossible to avoid. Even though I did cycle up iconic Italian climbs, and the heat was ridiculous, they were both made a little easier by the many viewing points we stopped at along the way. The valleys were beautiful: there was a stark contrast between the fertile meadows and harsh, "industrial" looking mountain range. Wildflowers drenched the landscape while providing bumblebees with a lifetime of work. Much to the delight of my inner "farmer's daughter," there were fat, brown cows wearing huge cow bells that gently chimed through the air.

While cycling the area was a huge challenge unfortunately it was very noisy too. There were gangs of tourists on big, heavy and most notably deafening motor bikes that whizzed past us at speed each day. They were frightening to deal with especially when I was on a very technical downhill that consisted of multiple switchbacks. It was hard enough to navigate the roads on my bike but with motorbikes coming at me from every angle I nearly peed in my pants with fear! At times they were so close to me I could taste the omissions from their engine. Other times as oncoming traffic, they were headed directly for me and then at the last minute they would swerve and narrowly avoid me. It was scary to say the least. It was such a pity that such a beautiful area and the peaceful mountains were being bombarded by stinky engines! In fairness though, the roads are a cyclist's dream which also makes them the perfect grand prix track for big engines too.

However it wasn't all bad. Before going on the trip, I had promised myself a quiet, "me day" for rest and relaxation and true to my word I waved my friends goodbye one day. They were going cycling, and I was going on a nature walk! I took a cable car high up into the most spectacular secluded valleys away from the roads and the terrifying motorbikes. As well as being incredibly peaceful, thankfully as the mountains were so high the temperature was a little more manageable too. I took a little stroll around the meadows and let the long grass tickle my bare legs. From such a height, I was able to pick out a section of the road I had cycled the previous day. It looked small in comparison to the large expansive vista before me. From where I was standing on the mountain top the road looked positively flat which I can assure you it was not. My aching legs were testimony to that. As I wandered around the meadow I inhaled the fresh air and enjoyed being "on top of the world." The sky seemed close enough that I tried to reach up and touch it, I wanted to shake hands with Mother Nature and thank her for such a special place.

In the mountain top café I bought the largest slice of pizza they had and enjoyed every morsel of it. For dessert I ordered the biggest ice cream I could fit in my two hands. While the temperature at the summit wasn't as bad as below in the town, it was still hot. My ice-cream was melting pretty fast but luckily from years of experience I was able to gobble it up quickly with minimal waste! After my Italian culinary feast, I flopped my weary body and very full stomach into a deck chair. For a few hours I happily soaked up the momentous scenery and thoroughly enjoyed being surrounded by nature. I people watched for a while which was highly amusing, and then had a much-needed snooze in the sun.

I was glad that I had not cancelled the trip. I would have been kicking myself if I had, especially after seeing how spectacular the area was. Luckily, thanks to my very balanced approach of cycling, rest and gelato there were no repercussions to my health from cycling such difficult terrain in the heat.

When we returned to Ireland, summer finished and gave way to Autumn. I didn't cycle so much that season. I wasn't bored, I just knew that my body needed a good "down season" after all I had put it through during the previous 12 months. Besides, it was time for me to plan another solo adventure, my December trip of a lifetime. My legs decided that enough was enough, a sunshine, "easy" trip was long overdue. The Caribbean was calling...

Chapter 17
Cigars, Castro, beaches and the Bay of Pigs. Cuba 2019

The pilot signalled to the cabin crew to prepare for landing in Havana. I was sitting beside the window and could see miles and miles of endless white beaches and turquoise waters surrounding the island of Cuba. It looked magnificent and I couldn't wait to spend three whole weeks exploring and sunning myself there. My impending trip was going to be focused on beach days, relaxation, culture and rest. Naturally there would be some cycling but on a commuter bike with a basket on the front.

The bustling city of Havana was my first stop. As usual, for my first day anywhere new, I immediately went looking for my fresh air and bike fix to help me recover from the long journey. I had flown from Amsterdam to Havana, and while it was a very comfortable 12-hour flight, I couldn't wait to stretch my legs and get outside into the sunshine. A city bike tour was required to help me immerse myself into Cuban life and acclimatise to the amazing weather.

Ditching my winter clothes for shorts, sandals and shades I was more than ready for my solo adventure in a tropical paradise. While December was the high season I was the only tourist that particular day looking to cycle through the old colonial city. I usually love cycling with others, but I was thrilled to have my own private tour just that once. I didn't have to wait around on slowcoaches who hadn't cycled in years or be the photographer for couples at every monument. (I don't mind doing that but sometimes it's nice to not be around loved-up couples or families.)

My guide was excited too, he loved having a single woman on his tour all to himself. He tried to show off to me by flexing some muscle on the first hill (really it was more like a bump in the road.) Unfortunately for him, he had no idea who he was trying to impress. Even though I was wearing sandals and melting with the heat, I powered on up the hill and left him for dust. It felt really good to make mince meat out of someone who just assumed that I was "a pretty lady on a bike!" (This could be why I am single though, I never let the guys win!)

In between periodic bike races with my guide, I enjoyed being free as a bird in the Caribbean. With the wind in my hair and the sun heating my body, we whizzed around the streets of Havana, dodging large open top Mustangs, Chevies, Thunderbirds and other amazing cars from the 1950s. I thought the colours in Myanmar were memorable but in Cuba the bright pink, electric blue, red and turquoise green convertible cars with white leather interiors were a technicolour feast for my eyes. They were polished to perfection and their chrome bumpers sparkled in the sun so brightly that they dazzled me as they drove around the streets. While they sparkled they challenged my ear drums too. The sound of their engines humming up the road was like a soft earthquake topped off with Cuban salsa music blaring from their stereos.

Cycling around Havana, I really appreciated how colonial it was, a melting pot of history and colour. Unfortunately though, the city was literally falling apart. The beautiful buildings were mostly crumbling and in need of a lot of love and attention. There was immense poverty and terribly neglected infrastructure, dwarfed at times by brand new, European 5-star Hotels. Usually, the sun and bright blue skies make everything look better but even the sorry state of Havana's once fine buildings could not be disguised.

No trip to Havana is complete without visiting Plaza de la Revolution. Cycling into the fine square, which was an incredible expanse of dull, grey concrete, I failed to notice the armed army officer chasing me. While I had to get a tourist permit to enter Cuba that was the first notable moment that I was reminded that Cuba was not the land of the free. It most definitely is a communist country where rules must be obeyed.

Apparently there was no cycling allowed in the exceptionally large, open, flat area. It was just begging for some trees, a time trial circuit or a skateboard park if you ask me! However, in Communist Cuba, it remained a place of compliance and most definitely, no fun on bikes. Sheepishly I got off my bike, waved an apology and disciplined myself abruptly. Who was I to argue with a gun-toting officer?

Che Guevara and Camilo Cienfuegos, two of Cuba's finest revolutionaries, overlooked the proceedings in the Plaza. Their images covered the full sides of two large concrete government buildings. There was also a very striking tower in the plaza, made of even more concrete. Only for the sun and the brightly coloured convertible cars parked there I would have thought I was in a black and white movie. While the tower was tall and imposing, to be honest I found it kind of obnoxious and phallic. It was a memorial to Jose Marti, another Cuban national hero and the place where Fidel Castro gave numerous public addresses to the poor citizens who had to stand in the heat below in the plaza. Compared to the beautiful coastline we had previously cycled along; Plaza de la Revolution was the epitome of drab 1970s architecture under military rule.

We finished off our tour at the National Capitol Building which looked like it had been transported directly from Washington DC. While they are very similar in design my guide was very proud to tell me that the Cuban dome was a metre higher than the one in the USA. It was the first of many times throughout the trip that Cubans would tell me how much better than the Americans they were. Who was I to disagree? After all, they seemed rather fond of machine guns, and I had no allegiance to the USA!

I loved my time in Havana, but I wanted to see as much of the country as I could and experience all that Cuba had to offer. The island was big, roughly the same length as Italy, however, getting around it was easy and a lot of fun thanks to "colectivos". They were shared tourist taxis, great big old cars, not like the shiny tourist ones in Havana. These were uncomfortable and noisy as hell when inside them. However they did the job and went like the clappers, even with 6 to 8 passengers and a tonne of luggage wedged into the trunk. The drivers reminded me of my hero taxi driver all those years before in Bolivia. They were super proud of their motors, even if they were jalopies!

After my few days in Havana, cigar country was next on my informal itinerary. I took a colectivo southwest, deep into the rural Cuban countryside, and arrived in the gorgeous quaint town of Viñales. It was a sleepy little town, renowned for Cuban cigars and tobacco plantations. The countryside was lovely, lush and green, with a valley of limestone hills. It was by far my favourite town in Cuba, rustic to say the least, with local men walking around in plaid shirts and denim, some even wearing Stetsons. They looked like proper ranchers. I didn't know whether to say "Hola" to them or give them a big "Yee Haw!"

I adored the relaxed atmosphere, good restaurants and laid-back vibe of Viñales. It felt peaceful and I was glad to be in the country and surrounded by farmland. Although the beaches in Cuba were out of this world, as you know I am a country girl at heart. I felt very much at home being surrounded by crops and livestock. As you've guessed, there was only one way to see the area, I rented a bike and cycled out of town to explore the valley and smoke cigars!

The bike that I hired was perfect for my day trip, there was even a basket on the front for my camera and naturally, my Snoopy teddy was onboard, sitting in the best spot. I think he was glad that we were doing something "normal" that year and he wouldn't have to listen to me swearing my head off. I often wonder if he could talk, would he ask to be rescued from travelling with me! (Surely not?)

While I had a map of the area I chose to just go with the flow and see where I wound up. That was the beauty of being on my own once again. I happily changed my mind and direction on a whim, and it made no difference to anyone else on the planet.

Pottering along on my bike I spotted a sign saying, "cigars for sale" and immediately took a detour down a rough lane. The owner waved when he saw me approaching; like every Cuban I met he was very friendly and welcoming. We entered his "cigar factory" which was a little shed at the side of his house. (By the way, Cuba is very safe, I was not in the slightest bit worried about being alone on the farm with him. Cubans are poor by our standards, and they just want to make a sale. Besides, I think they have strict rules there judging by the military and number of guns I saw.) I really appreciated that the owner took time out from his day to show me his land which was filled with healthy, green tobacco plants. He generously launched into his spiel and explained to me the entire process of how a tobacco leaf eventually becomes a cigar. There was just one small problem. He only spoke Spanish at the speed of light and his accent was very difficult for me to understand, in fact I had no idea whatsoever what he was saying.

I politely smiled at the "good" parts of the story when he seemed to be very enthusiastic and laughing at something. Finishing off his lesson he pulled a huge cigar from his breast pocket and asked me if I would like to smoke it. I understood that! I couldn't say no. Snipping off the end he popped it in his mouth and lit it for me. He was trying to get it going and was smacking his lips around it; he looked like a goldfish, opening and closing his mouth without inhaling or swallowing anything. He motioned for me to take it. I had never smoked a cigar in my entire life. I knew not to inhale it but likewise I didn't actually know how to smoke it. I tried one of his goldfish impressions and that seemed to make him very happy. He smiled brightly and gave me a big thumbs-up.

I have no idea how people enjoy cigars. It was beyond disgusting. I instantly turned green and felt sick as a dog. I wanted to sluice my mouth out with bleach and my stomach was suddenly churning. I could not get rid of the taste in my mouth for days: even tabasco didn't work for me. It was completely vile but let's be honest, I couldn't go to Cuba and not try one. Maybe they were not high-quality Cuban cigars or perhaps I am just not cultured enough to appreciate them. I didn't care either way as I wont be doing that again! I did buy some off the plantation owner to support his business and they made perfect gifts for friends and family back home.

Cycling through the remote countryside I discovered numerous other small farms along the dusty roads. Most were growing crops and had chickens running free. I stumbled upon lovely viewpoints and waved to local farmers working their land. Cycling along the dirt tracks orange dust kicked up and attached itself to my feet and my open toe sandals. My feet were filthy, I was hot and sweaty and yet, I was happy as a pig in muck!

When I was stopped at a little bar, a very handsome cowboy in a check shirt and Stetson hat proceeded to chat me up. He was rugged and manly, covered in just the right amount of stubble, and tanned. He was even chomping on a Cuban cigar for added masculinity and authenticity. He was the real deal and I have to admit, I did swoon! My Spanish was good enough to have a flirtatious conversation with him, even if the language barrier had been a problem, the twinkle in his eye said it all. He had horses and wanted to take me on a trek to a lake for a swim. It sounded idyllic and I was honestly tempted. He was so dishy and macho and smelt like someone who knew how to work hard. While I really wanted to go on a horse and have a swim with him, much to my regret my "sensible" side took over. I turned down his generous offer and continued to cycle alone (while instantly regretting my decision)!

I soaked up the tranquillity of the valley and found my days were wonderfully stress-free. Since I had arrived in Cuba my phone was turned off most of the time and boy was I glad of the peace and quiet. My network at home didn't even have a roaming plan for Cuba and Wi-Fi was extremely limited. I must admit that being forced to unplug, have a detox from social media and be off the radar for a few weeks was no hardship at all. There was internet in Cuba: it was very limited, and I had to queue up for an hour or more at the government agency to buy "credits" to use it.

However, there was always the "black market" which I was very happy to support. I didn't care that I had to pay a little more for my internet credits as I was happy to help a budding entrepreneur. Besides, I got to practise my Spanish with the street vendor, so it was a win-win for us both. They always asked me about my life, my country and all the places that I had visited that they would never have the chance to see.

In comparison to the locals I had freedom to travel and a passport that is readily accepted all over the world. I had the money to buy my airfares and a fancy phone that is just an everyday object to me. I also had a lot more opportunities than them and most importantly, I had freedom of speech which is something that I rarely thought about until I was in a communist country. I can stand up and shout for a cause that is dear to me, make waves and use my vote to change our country as I see fit. Don't get me wrong; of course we have our own economic and cultural issues, but when I witnessed first-hand the Cuban way of life, I definitely appreciated which side my bread was buttered on. Gladly I bought my internet credit on the "black market" and never haggled over the price. It was only pennies to me, yet a big help to them.

I was more present on that trip than I had been on most of my other trips. Not since the ashram in India had I had so few distractions, and I noticed how much it benefited me. I was able to enjoy listening to nothing and be completely in the moment. Feeling the sunshine wrap around my body, I felt very happy that I had been transported back to the 1950's.

From the countryside in Viñales I squeezed into another colectivo with five other tourists and our luggage. From the west coast of Cuba we drove east along the south coast. My number one aim was to lie flat on my back on pure white sand and do nothing for a few days.

Having left winter firmly behind in Europe the Caribbean coast was heaven-sent, along with the longer hours of daylight each day. The beaches that I visited were nothing like the photos I had seen on the internet; in reality, they were a million times better. I walked across soft, bright white powder sand that was so fine it was impossible to pick up or make a sandcastle with - I did try!

I made sure on my Cuban odyssey to take lots of seaside rest days. Unlike my trip to Colombia where I tried to see and do everything, Cuba was the opposite. Plus I had to admit to myself that I was getting older, (I was 46 at that time), and my body was shouting very loudly that it needed and wanted a lot more breaks. For once I was willing to cooperate and sunbathe. Besides, I hadn't come all the way across the Atlantic Ocean to miss a once in a lifetime opportunity to do absolutely nothing on some of the most beautiful beaches I had ever seen.

Those days with rest and relaxation as well as peace and quiet allowed my inner thoughts and feelings to come bubbling up to the surface. Being alone and rested was actually a lot more productive than being busy with others. My mind and heart once again began to fill with hopes, dreams and love for the future. At times, out of the blue, my head suddenly went into overdrive with creativity, ideas, planning, goal setting and inspiration. It was like a volcano of ideas that was continually erupting in my head. That was when I started to scribble notes for this book. One day I cycled from the city of Trinidad to Playa Ancon which wasn't far at all. I was lying on the most fabulous pure white beach which was lined with palm trees. Even though it was a weekend, and the locals were a little noisy, I happily let myself daydream and think about all kinds of things, especially my past, present and future. Under the blue skies with a fresh coconut in my hand I took out a pen and paper, old school style, and vigorously jotted down all my thoughts⊠..these ones! I decided that day to draft a book to inspire others which was a lot more difficult than I ever anticipated. I spent the next few weeks making notes at every given opportunity. In fact, writing gave me a new passion, sitting down!

My journey around Cuba brought me to Playa Larga, a tiny town on the Bay of Pigs which had more gorgeous beaches. When planning my trip I made sure to include the bay on my itinerary, not just because it was where the CIA invaded in 1961, but because my dad was a pig farmer and I thought it would be fun to send him a photo from there. While there were no actual pigs running around, it was a very quaint and quiet town. The only disruption to the peace was when the vegetable man came around each morning with his horse and cart, shouting that he and his fresh produce had arrived. (Like I said, time has stood still in Cuba: there are no huge western style supermarkets, and even though there are shops there is absolutely nothing in them. I mean that. Empty shelves greeted me at the door, freezer cabinets were plugged in and running with absolutely nothing inside them. Cuba was the only place on the planet where locals sheepishly whispered, "have you any clothes for me?")

During my few days in Playa Largo I stayed with an immensely kind family who had a very up-market casa. They generously invited me and all of their guests to a spit roast pig dinner on Christmas eve. Normally I wouldn't thank you for pork but given that this was the Bay of Pigs, a Christmas feast and a personal invite from the family, I ate my festive dinner without fuss. I was amazed at how delicious the salty, crispy, crackling that had formed on the skin was. It was neither greasy nor soggy; the pig had been cooked to perfection for hours on a rotisserie. I devoured it. When my host kindly offered me seconds I didn't hesitate which is unheard of for me and pork. Not only was their feast amazing, but the company was also excellent. Enthusiastically they taught me how to salsa dance Cuban style. I loved being twirled, pushed and pulled as my dance partner took the reins and gave me some much-needed discipline. For once I wasn't in charge and I relished the moment.

For my Christmas Day adventure I chose to cycle the whole way around the Bay of Pigs from Playa Larga to Playa Giron. The man in my Casa made it his business to hire me "the best bike in town." In reality it was more like the only bike in the town but what could I do? Like I said, choice is limited on the island so I could either take it or leave it. I took it!

Setting off on my purple steed for the day all I could do was hope for the best while riding it. It was a little rusty, the chain and cassette were also parched of oil and squeaking. At least the front brake worked, however, while the bike may have had ten speeds, only three were operational. Overall the bike was pretty uncomfortable but all in all it would do the job of getting me around the Bay of Pigs.

My destination, Playa Giron and the Museo de la Intervencion (the victory museum celebrating how the Cubans stopped the CIA invasion to overthrow Castro in 1961), was a mere thirty-six kilometres away. As you know by now I am a strong cyclist but a seventy-two-kilometre round trip on a jalopy was even a bit ambitious by my standards. However, just like my cycle in Myanmar, I had all day to potter around and as usual it actually never occurred to me to find another form of transport or an alternative, easier adventure.

The Caribbean scenery was stunning. I cycled along the coast which was lined the whole way with beautiful palm trees. The Caribbean Sea was the most beautiful turquoise green I had ever seen and with the sun reflecting off it, it looked like a large blanket of sparkling diamonds. Tootling along, I had my phone shoved down the front of my bra and was playing 90's house music very loudly. It was just me, Snoopy and the open road for the day. I felt extremely safe and secure on my bike as there were next to no other road users. It was a real treat not having to worry about being run over! The odd time a big old car drove by me they gave me a little "hello" beep which prompted us to wave enthusiastically at each other.

My cycle down the coast was very pleasant but boy was I glad when I reached the museum. It was well worth the trip even though my legs were feeling wrecked from cycling such an old bike to get there. I was a bit sore too as I had some chafing in my inner thighs which was not exactly pleasant. I would live though. I was a seasoned cyclist, who had already accumulated numerous physical and emotional scars from cycling. One more was not going to kill me.

Staggering around the Museum, I was trying to look at the pictures and artefacts without keeling over as my legs had decided to turn to jelly. I periodically gave them little slaps to try and get them to work. The entire museum was in Spanish, and I could understand some of it but even if I had not, I could feel the enormity of the Cubans' pride at beating the CIA. It was oozing from every picture and artifact. The museum was a showcase for their artillery as well as the remains of the American airplanes they had shot down. While I liked the exhibition, it was a bit of a contradiction to be spending Christmas day looking at grenades, machine guns and rocket launchers! Admittedly it wasn't very festive of me, but on the other hand I was glad that the museum was open that day. It fitted into my itinerary perfectly and I was able to learn a little more about Cuba's modern history and the weaponry they were so fond of.

After my educational museum visit I cycled slowly a little further along the coast to find a beach stop. I didn't have to go very far or look that hard, after all I was on the south coast of Cuba. I parked my bike at the most wonderful sandy beach cove, Playa Coco. It was a glorious place to set up camp for the day and celebrate Christmas in my own unique way.

Stretching out my towel under the straw parasol, I carefully unwrapped my tiny, travel-size Christmas tree and popped it in the sand. Never one to miss an adventure, Snoopy sat smack bang in the middle of my beach towel. Last but not least, I popped on my dangly Christmas earrings and I was all set for my little beach party. I swam, ate and snoozed. It was the perfect Christmas day in my opinion.

I was sad when the time came to leave the beach. However, I was grateful to have had another wonderful Christmas somewhere exotic. Luckily, my legs were feeling a little livelier thanks to their minimal exertion on the sand. Once the bike was loaded up and Snoopy was back onboard, we began our return journey to Playa Largo.

Earlier on in the day, while cycling around the bay to the museum, I passed a snorkelling cove with a juice bar. It was a hive of activity and I had earmarked it in order to have a little pit stop on my return journey. It looked like the "in "place to be as there were lots of other tourists there, milling around soaking up the sun.

Cycling back was easier as I had my little break stamped in my brain. It broke up the journey nicely for me and gave me something to look forward to. I was right about the pit stop. The refreshment bar was cute and naturally there was Cuban music blaring from a speaker on the counter. There were lots of other tourists still there, lounging around on the grass bank sipping drinks. Even though it was the high season, "real" Cuba was not exactly busy. (The all-inclusive resorts are full in December.) It was nice to see that there were plenty of other travellers who, like me, had opted to be an independent tourist and see what Cuba is really like.

I stood my bike up against the back of the shack shop and with just a few footsteps I was at the water's edge. (Luckily I had done my research and had brought my snorkel to Cuba too.) I launched into the amazing crystal-clear Caribbean waters and entered another world. A conveyor belt of all kinds of colourful fish came swimming by. The sun shone through the water, illuminating the entire seabed and made the fish look even more beautiful to me. I could see their unique colours, shapes, and sizes very clearly. I had snorkelled in many other exotic locations in the past, including Thailand, the great barrier reef, Fiji and Mauritius, but somehow this little cove in the Bay of Pigs made a bigger impression on me than any of them. I'm sure it was due to the fact that I was in such a good place within myself. I had matured and accepted myself fully. I also didn't have to impress anyone or for that matter be accountable to anyone. I was having a great day and genuinely didn't need or want for anything on the planet. I was content with my life and at that moment, I was the richest person on the planet.

While I was snorkelling, I was being careful not to disturb the fish. (I was a visitor to their world after all.) Despite my traumatic sinking to the bottom of the pool as a child in the Canaries, I absolutely adore snorkelling. I felt perfectly safe with my face stuck in the water while my arms and legs flapped around. I knew that I was not going to be mistaken for a mermaid any time soon, but I was proud that I had overcome my fear of the water and was able to enjoy a little moment of "fish life."

Never in all my life, on any cycle anywhere in the world have I enjoyed my "tea break" as much. That pit stop made up for all the cold, soggy cycles in crazy high winds that I have endured in the depths of Irish winters. When myself and my friends stop on our coffee break we must gulp down our drinks really fast to avoid getting hypothermia. The mad thing is, we call that fun and think it's "normal." I never, ever, in all my life imagined that one day I would stop mid cycle, pop on my snorkel, and swim with tropical fish. It was honestly the highlight of my entire trip.

Having changed back into my "cycling" clothes, shorts and vest, I was ready for the last leg of my mammoth cycle on my jalopy. I tied my wet bikini to the rack at the back of the bike and tried to create a little washing line so they would dry quickly on the way home.

Back on the road, I was tootling along on my bike and feeling very satisfied with my day. I had my music on once again and was singing loudly, enjoying life, when suddenly, without warning my bike came to an abrupt stop and I nearly went flying over the handlebars.

My bikini bottoms had fallen off the rack and were caught up in the cogs and bike chain. Goddammit! They were wedged down deeply, in a ferocious tangle and I couldn't free them from the mechanisms. The pedals were completely stuck, and the bike was totally immobilized. There was no way I could ride the bike another centimetre further. How the hell was I going to fix it? It was going to be a very long walk home to Playa Largo. No matter how hard I pulled at my bottoms they simply would not budge. "F**K!"

Luckily, it wasn't that long before a helpful man drove towards me. His great big 1950's motorcar was so noisy that at first I thought it was a Boeing 747 coming down the road. While I was temporarily deafened I was extremely glad he was slowing down and stopping to help me.

I didn't have the Spanish to explain my problem exactly to him, but when I pointed to my bikini and made a worried face he got the idea. Like a superhero he jumped out of the car, flipped the bike upside down and without any effort at all, he duly ripped my bikini bottoms free from the chain. I was so relieved and then instantly mortified as he waved my bottoms around while he explained to me that they were the problem. (I was aware of that!)

Even though he was having a little chuckle at my expense, and I was mortified, he kindly checked the bike over for me. He rotated the pedals a few times and squeezed the brakes. He gave me a thumbs up to assure me that it was working properly again. I was relieved that the bike was functional again even though my bikini was ruined. After thanking him profusely in my very best Spanish, I jumped back on my jalopy and sped off as fast as I could.

185

As if my clothing ordeal weren't bad enough, I could see the sun starting to drop from the sky. In Cuba there was little to no dusk as I was so close to the equator. I had to cycle faster. The sun was trying to outdo me and appeared to have picked up its speed too. It dropped rapidly under the horizon and beat me in our race. I had a fair idea that I was near Playa Largo, but I couldn't be 100% sure exactly how far it was. I was cycling even more frantically as it was fully dark, and I didn't have any lights on my bike. While there was very little traffic, there were no streetlights either.

I was totally knackered when I eventually rolled back into the small town which thankfully had a few lights on. I was relieved to cycle up the last road to my Casa and finally get off the most uncomfortable saddle in the world. There was even a welcoming committee out to greet me in the form of mosquitos. Naturally, I got attacked by them. All of them in fact!

After my few days of fun in Playa Larga I took a bus from the south coast all the way to the north coast. I was spending my final days in Cuba on the beach of Varadero. (Renowned, fabulous beach from the travel brochures.) Unfortunately, the bus was an hour late but that's life in Cuba, you just have to accept it and move on. No sooner had I sat down and made myself comfortable for the journey, when suddenly the bus swerved violently. Everyone screamed as we hurtled across to the other side of the road, and skidded for gosh knows how long before eventually coming to an abrupt halt. We had collided with a tourist on a motorbike who luckily was OK apart from cuts and bruises.

While it was frightening there was no panic by the bus driver, or by any of the locals for that matter. I was amused by their casual approach to the traffic accident. The forensics team eventually came with a measuring tape like the one I had in my toolbox at home. They also had a pen, paper and calculator to work out the braking distance. The police arrived at the scene and set up a "major" traffic diversion. They had one traffic cone between them and stood smoking cigarettes while waving at the few cars that came along the scene to go around the coach. Meanwhile all the tourists on the bus, myself included, got out and had a wander around the road which was closed for technical examination!

After two hours the bus was finally cleared by forensics to continue its journey. The bus driver was totally unfazed by the incident. He resumed his seat behind the steering wheel and told us to sit down. There was no litigation, whiplash, shock, trauma counselling or PTSD from the diver or the passengers. No one cared about any of that, we just wanted to get to the beach! We resumed our journey and our driver kindly drove as fast as he could to make up for lost time. Eventually (and safely) we pulled into the bus station on the idyllic north coast.

I spent five well deserved days relaxing on the most amazing beach. It was idyllic to say the least. I spent my time writing, snoozing, swimming, tanning, doing nothing and loving every minute of it. It was the perfect ending to the trip and the decade. 2020 was just a few days away and I was totally refreshed and revitalized to welcome it in.

To see one decade out and say hello to another, I spent midnight on New Year's skinny dipping in the gloriously warm, calm sea under the moon and all the stars above. It felt like I was washing away the old and was feeling super optimistic for my future. As I floated on my back in the warm water, looking up to the heavens, I made a wish. I knew that whoever was up above listening to me that night, would hear my desires and help me in every way possible to have whatever I wanted.

I could not wait to get the ball rolling with my newfound motivation, determination and renewed energy. I was one hundred percent positive that 2020 was going to be even better than my action packed 2019. I even wrote in my journal, in big fancy italics, "Watch out world here I come!"

"Unexpected events can set you back or set you up. It's all a matter of perspective."

-*Mary Anne Radmacher*

Chapter 18
A dramatic turn of events
2020

I was excited for life and hit the ground running in January. I was glowing with Cuban sunshine and was super annoying to all who met me! Businesswise I was invigorated, enthusiastic to push my limits, learn new skills, improve my Spanish and get help from mentors. I was a powerhouse of motivation and loved every minute of it.

In March, once again I touched down in Spain for my annual cycling week with Cormac. As I stepped off of the plane, instantly I felt the warmth penetrating my bones and regenerating my inner solar panels. Unfortunately though, as soon as I passed through arrivals the authorities told me that the country was going into an emergency lockdown, with immediate effect. Overnight life changed rapidly for all of us and there was not a single thing we could do about it.

My wonderful cycling week was cancelled, and I had no choice but to pay €300 for a flight back to Ireland which also went into lockdown! I wasn't worried though, since we were assured that it was a temporary measure, and it was only going to be for a few weeks at the most. Life would resume and it would all be "grand." As luck would have it, much to everyone's delight and surprise Ireland had an unexpected heatwave too. How lucky was that?

While I was concerned about keeping my parents safe and obviously didn't want to catch Covid myself, I was more than willing to find alternative ways to work and continue writing my book. I had to get my Yoga classes online urgently and become a technical wizard overnight. It wasn't easy, but it really was a case of sink or swim. I pushed all the furniture down to one end of my sitting room and created a suitable Yoga backdrop. Overnight, like every other household, my home became my office, living quarters and holiday refuge.

The first week of lockdown was brilliant. Thanks to the warm weather and the sun shining I enjoyed pottering around my garden. I also did a big de-clutter which felt very cathartic. The only real concern that I had was finding a way to stay super fit during lockdown as I had an impending cycling trip to the Pyrenees in France. I really couldn't afford to go mad on ice-cream and sit around all day in the sun. Thanks to my healthy mindset, hitting the bottle and consuming copious amounts of alcohol never crossed my mind. Even though I knew that half the country were having barbeques and "larging it up," that was something I could not and absolutely would not do to myself. Thankfully I wasn't even remotely tempted but I did wonder about others who may not have been as strong willed.

My training for France was going well before lockdown. However the rules that were imposed on us during that time were not at all training-friendly. (We were only allowed to exercise inside a 2-kilometre radius from our homes.) For me there was no point cycling under those terms and conditions. I had to find another way to keep active and physically strong as well as creating my daily fix of happy hormones.

I needed Jane Fonda! My old friend in her leotard was the only person who could help me at home. Her keep fit exercises were online and I couldn't wait to relive my youth. Seeing her on my TV with her big, poofy hair and tiny waist made me feel like I had my best friend at home with me. I must admit, I went completely over top with exercise as there wasn't a whole lot else to do. Inspired by Jane I put on an online fitness festival for my own customers. I hoped that I could help them to stay sane and fit the same way she was helping me. Even though my classes were over Zoom it gave us all an opportunity to have "live" chats with others as well as giving me a valuable reason to get up every day.

One day we were bouncing around our sitting rooms like lunatics, giving it all we had in a boxing style class. We were pretending to punch the crap out of imaginary opponents, (great stress relief) squatting, doing push ups and "kick boxing." We were absolutely going for it. The music was blaring, and I was shouting orders. On my screen I could see everyone enthusiastically following my every word. They were bobbing up and down, coordinated with me in their kitchens and sitting rooms. At one point we were pretending to skip with an imaginary jump rope when out of the blue, BANG!

I didn't know what had happened or where the noise came from. I thought perhaps that I had broken a floorboard. Looking around me I was trying to find the damage when suddenly I keeled over, live on air.

I had snapped my Achilles tendon; the loud bang was it rupturing which brought an abrupt end to my very short lived "boxing" career. My foot was floppy, just dangling at the end of my leg. I couldn't control or move it at all, let alone try to stand on it. I was mid class and had a screen full of people waiting for me to tell them what to do next. Not being one to let my fan club down I kept going. Even though I couldn't stand up there was no reason why we couldn't do stomach and bum exercises on the floor. I wasn't in any pain and honestly, at the time, I didn't think the injury was that bad. After an hour and a lot of sweat I logged off, assessed my ankle properly and immediately rang an ambulance.

It was hard to believe that while trying to obey the rules and "do the right thing" amid a pandemic, I ended up on the operating table with multiple stitches and a blue cast.

At first I was so annoyed with myself. I was upset that while I was trying to do some good for myself and others it had backfired on me. It didn't seem at all fair. However it wasn't the first time I had ended up in a cast - I'd broken my other leg in 2012 on an adventure race while running down a hill in Wicklow. I knew that with extreme workouts comes a risk, but I never expected a home workout to debilitate me. If I had jumped out of a plane or done something really crazy then I would say, "fair enough." At least I knew from my past experience on crutches how to manage my injury and what I needed to do for my recovery. There was no other way around it, I had to sit down and wait 6-8 weeks for my leg to heal.

The Covid restrictions didn't last a couple of weeks, they rolled on and on and on. While it did not make any odds to me as my mobility was limited I started to find it very difficult to smile. I had lost my one big, happy hormone-producing outlet and my hope of cycling the Pyrenees were completely dashed. April crept by as did most of May. My parents couldn't come to visit me as they were cocooning and while my sister, friends and neighbours were very good to me, I missed basic things such as buying my own food.

Even though I was doing my best to stay upbeat, it was getting harder and harder to find the motivation to get up in the mornings let alone leave my house for an outdoor meeting with a friend. I was sure I wasn't the only one feeling hopeless and thought that perhaps the "cure" was far worse than the illness.

While many years had passed since my trip inside the four walls for my own safety, as time went on I became concerned for my welfare because of the negative impact lockdown was having on my mental health. I was very aware of the death toll as well as the stress it was causing the entire world, but I was very angry that fit, healthy people were expected to sit at home and "do nothing" while shops were having bumper sales with alcohol. I was livid in fact. I felt very strongly that the importance of exercise, healthy eating and mental health were completely overlooked at that time. There was no mention of self-care or positivity on the news, radio or the TV adverts. It was as if all of the above were actively being discouraged and no one cared that a large proportion of the nation were becoming junk food addicts and alcohol- dependent. I was discouraged by those in charge to say the least. I felt extremely upset by the entire situation and could clearly see the long-term mental-health repercussions of lockdown that no one, not even the "experts", was thinking about.

The only silver lining was that as each day passed my injury got better. It healed perfectly, much faster than the doctors expected. By the time I got signed off by the hospital in early June, the restrictions were slowly beginning to ease just a little bit. Even though international travel was still banned, and I couldn't buy anything other than food, hardware items and a truck load of alcohol (if I wanted it), I was happy to be able to walk again and visit the supermarket for myself.

By mid-June I was fully recovered and while all cycling events were cancelled the roads and mountains were very much open for enjoyment. I went cycling as much as I could for the rest of the summer and was reunited with my cycling friends. Finally, fun and laughter were back on the menu.

Autumn crept in, nature changed colours and the leaves on the trees gently let go and floated onto the road. My warm cycling gloves and hat were called back into action. Along with the day, our cycling routes became shorter and shorter. Luckily, there were still hot cups of tea available to drink on our breaks.

Gradually the days got even darker. My jumpers got thicker, and the old familiar dread of winter that I had avoided for years with my annual December trips abroad started to creep back in.

I could have stayed in Ireland all winter long and battled through the eternal darkness that winter brought to both daylight and my head, but that was a challenge I was not willing to risk. I had enough of the relentless bad news, on the radio, TV and in every conversation I listened to. My opinions hadn't changed, I was 100% anti lockdown on the grounds of severe damage to the nation's mental health. Don't get me wrong, it was serious, and people were dying, but what about those who were living? There was no mention of them.

While life may not have returned to "normal" one thing had drastically changed for the better. The airport was open, and planes were taking off daily. I needed to get the heck out of Ireland and get some winter sunshine, pandemic or not.

Chapter 19
The Valley of the Tears
Gran Canaria 2020

I didn't walk into the airport, I sprinted! Even though there were very few people travelling at that time I paid extra for "FastTrack" security so that I could get airside in double quick time. I wanted to drop to my knees and kiss the floor when I was reunited with my beloved departure area. The shops were open, there was life and activity. Everything was just as it should be. After I bought my cup of tea and juicy gossip magazine, I made a beeline for my departure gate to make absolutely sure that I was first in the boarding queue.

Gran Canaria was my chosen destination for winter 2020. While I would have preferred to go further afield it was not a possibility at that time. We were "allowed" to travel within Europe so long as it was for essential purposes. I ticked that box confidently. It was essential to my mental health and wellbeing.

The Canary Islands were the perfect solution for winter sunshine and escapism. Luke, a friend of mine from my cycling club, was going there for a weeklong cycling holiday and I managed to wrangle an invitation to join him. (Admittedly it was more that I persuaded him to let me tag along!)

We each had our own apartment, which was an ideal set up for both of us, being together but separate. Happily, we both came and went as we pleased as we were not tied to each other in any way. What I loved most about my time with Luke was, it was easy. If we met up for dinner, great, if we didn't there was no problem. We had no expectations of each other and therefore neither of us was ever disappointed. We were the perfect travel duo in my eyes.

Gran Canaria was perfect too. There was glorious sunshine and warm temperatures. There was also many extra hours of daylight, a warm sea to swim in, tough cycling routes, and best of all, there were day trips on boats and eating al fresco. I was in heaven.

Luke had been to the island many times before and was happy to oversee all of our cycling route planning and coffee stops. As I was simply tagging along on his trip, I was more than willing to cooperate and ride whatever routes he picked. I was just delighted to be there and forget about Covid for a week. I really didn't care what we did or where we went so long as it was outdoors, on a bike and in the sun. My number one goal for the trip was to get as much sunshine and vitamin D as humanly possible. I was determined to boost my immune system and get a tan in winter.

On the very first morning of my holiday, I jumped enthusiastically out of bed and ran at top speed down to the beach. It was like a scene from a movie, I was running and undressing at the same time, throwing off my clothes (apart from my bikini) and letting them fall behind me. I didn't care in the slightest where they landed or if I ever saw them again! I ran straight into the sea and kept going until it was deep enough to submerge myself fully under the waves. When I popped my head up out of the water I was overcome with happiness to see the glorious sunshine and golden beach.

The locals were dismayed at the "crazy" lady who was splashing around in the "cold" sea as if she were in the Caribbean. It wasn't cold to me, far from it, it was positively hot. (All through summer and winter, to rehab my Achilles, I had made regular trips to the Irish Sea which was freezing on a good day!) Lying on my back, bobbing around in the sea, I was looking upwards at the beautiful blue sky in the early morning brightness. Once again my body was free of winter woollies and my mind was finally liberated from anxiety. It was as if a huge weight had fallen off my shoulders: my whole body instantly softened, and every last ounce of tension washed away with the waves. I was thrilled to be somewhere new and over the moon to have a whole week of adventure ahead of me. I was very aware of how lucky I was to be there and vowed to myself that I would enjoy every second of every day.

Over breakfast Luke took me though our cycling itinerary and announced that on our last day we would be cycling the notorious Valley of the Tears. It was a renowned cycling route in Gran Canaria and has been featured in all the cycling magazines. It was dubbed as an "all-time, must do bucket list climb." Surprisingly, I had never heard of it but that was okay. Luke said that I could chalk it up as my annual crazy cycling challenge of epic proportions. I was worried by the name of the route as it suggested a lot of pain would be involved. While I am not one to shy away from suffer-fests I was apprehensive of going mad on that trip. I didn't want my brand-new Achilles tendon to rupture again.

Our first ride was short in distance, but it was by no means a walk in the park. It turned out that the island was very hilly even along the coast. On the plus side there were plenty of places open selling massive ice creams.

There were so many flavours to choose from: my eyes were overwhelmed by the different colours and textures as I scanned the ice cream buffet behind chilled glass. Each one looked more appetizing than the next. As I couldn't decide, there was only one thing to do - have two scoops. I had one scoop of black cherry and another of dark chocolate, yum! Luke and myself sat in the sunshine devouring our treats while looking at some very fine yachts bobbing around the harbour. While being a millionaire and owning a boat would be nice, I had learnt over the last ten months what truly mattered to me. I didn't need a huge bank balance or diamonds galore, I just needed to be free to travel, have friends and family nearby, and be healthy enough to enjoy myself along the way.

Our second cycling route brought us up to the famous Pico las Nieves, the second highest peak on the island. With beautiful sweeping views of the entire island, the summit sat almost dead centre of Gran Canaria. As I cycled my way to the summit, sweat was pouring off me and I struggled badly to get there. I would love to tell you that my hardship was due to the heat, or the severity of the climb but in truth the real reason I struggled was because there was a lot more of me than usual. Four kilograms (9lbs) more to be exact.

Like most people in lockdown, even for all the exercise I was doing, I had still managed to put on weight, especially around my stomach. I kept convincing myself that it was due to my age and hormones. However, when I tried lugging my excess baggage up a steep hill on a bike I finally had to admit that the real reason I had put on so much weight was due to comfort eating, stress and boredom. I was under no illusion that the two scoops of ice cream I had eaten the previous day were not exactly diet friendly, but surely they didn't count as I was on a cycling holiday.

For our final cycling day on the island, as planned, we set our computer maps to navigate us to the Valley of the Tears. Luke was super confident that we were both fit enough to complete the challenge and promised me that it would be a great day out. Just to reiterate the importance of completing the route he reminded me that if we did, it would give us both huge bragging rights for years to come! I definitely wanted to notch up another incredible cycling route on my "been there, done that" list.

The first segment of our grand tour was interesting and a little unexpected. Part of the coast road was closed as it had collapsed off of the cliff and fallen into the sea! There were two detours we could take. One was to sneak up onto the motorway and cycle to the next exit as fast as we could on the hard shoulder and pick up our route once again without any extra mileage. Option two was to turn back and cycle halfway around the island and eventually get back on course. This detour would add on hours, more hills and a lot of extra kilometres to the route.

The choice was simple. To be honest, we never hesitated with our decision. The route was going to be tough enough and we didn't need to add to our hardship. Sheepishly, we cycled up the ramp to the hard shoulder of the motorway. In our defence, we were only going one junction to the very end of the motorway. It was safe as the vehicles on the motorway were coming to a progressive slow-down and with the Covid crisis there was next to no traffic on the motorway to worry about. In fact the entire island was a ghost town. I felt a little flutter of nerves about breaking the rules of the road but at the same time I loved being a rebel with a brass neck who was up to no good. I felt giddy, bold and defiant all in one pedal stroke.

I absolutely do not condone breaking the rules of the road in any country even though I did. What's worse is I can't exactly say I am ashamed of it either. Cycling on a super flat, slick, fast surface are what cycling dreams are made of and sprinting down it was just too good an opportunity to miss. My heart was racing, I am not sure if it was from the risk of getting caught, or the adrenaline rush from being a bad girl.

I zoomed along the hard shoulder of the motorway, for just six hundred metres, as fast as my little legs would go. Pushing my heart and lungs to capacity, I bombed down the road at ludicrous speed trying to make the short section the ultimate time trial of my life.

The motorway naturally came to an end, and I exited on the off ramp. While I had the thrill of a lifetime I was glad to be back on the "normal" road and transform back into a law-abiding citizen. Thankfully, I had broken the rules without any police sirens or helicopters with tv cameras buzzing overhead. I was not an outlaw; I was a rebel.

From there we were back on course which took us twenty kilometres west to La Aldea de San Nicolás, a quaint little village high up in the hills on the west side of Gran Canaria. After a much-needed lunch break we headed into a canyon to begin the infamous Valley of The Tears.

The route was perfectly named. The road was ridiculously steep, and it was beyond punishing, which was not helped by the fact that it was in the middle of nowhere! The scenery was like a western movie, with red dust and dry canyons. It was extremely barren and very quiet. Luke and I each had our own cycling strengths but on hills I was just a little stronger. We agreed that we would cycle our own "race" and regroup at the end of the valley.

Once again, I was doing what I do best, suffering on a tough climb. Sometimes I wonder if I am a masochist or have some sort of addiction to putting myself through hell. My usual flood of swear words started to fall from my mouth which made me giggle. Needless to say, Snoopy was in my back pocket enjoying the ride. He was happily taking note of the new and improved curses I was producing. While I was overheating, irritable and in the middle of nowhere, there was no way I could have skipped cycling a "must do" route when it was on our doorstep.

The route was relentless but thankfully I wasn't exhausted. The day before we had gone on a fabulous catamaran trip. We swam in the ocean and rested on the deck. I was very glad to have had such a wonderful "day off" given how gruelling the Valley of the Tears was turning out to be.

Unfortunately, the valley just kept on giving. On and on it went, ambling around the canyon, up, down, and around. There were some impressive vistas to keep my mind occupied, and just when I thought I was through the worst of it, the fun began all over again.

The thoughts inside my head were not doing so well on that route. I was imagining the engineers who built the road were on front of me and I was giving them an earful about their design. I was even disgusted with "God" for not putting a drinking water fountain in the desert!

I think my head was in a spin due to a combination of the stress we had all endured for the last six months, or perhaps I was frustrated by my lack of fitness and extra body weight. It didn't matter what caused those thoughts, but at least when I became aware of them and realised that my head was out of control I was able to separate myself from them and see them for what they were. Having that awareness and hearing how ridiculous my conversations were made me chuckle. I was especially proud of my colourful vocabulary. I told my ego to shut up and stop whinging. I gave "her" a lot of reassurance that it was ok. It's not like we were lost or dying of hunger, we were doing OK. I reminded her that unlike Colombia, there were no vultures watching us and besides, we had been through a lot worse and survived.

Being able to stop myself in full "meltdown" and bring myself back into the moment was my saving grace that day. While the route didn't get any easier, when I got my head out of the chaos it was in, I slowed my bike down and took a kinder approach to the route. Instead of being on a tortuous, relentless cycle I was able to turn it into a sightseeing expedition. I even put on my 90's dance music and sang loudly (badly) which cheered me up no end.

Eventually, much to my relief, after two hours on a very long and lonely road I came to a viewpoint that was almost at the end of the canyon. I just had to complete one more downhill section which was going to be followed by a short climb that would finally take me to the canyon "exit." As I paused for a moment and enjoyed the vista an apparition appeared before my eyes.

Four lovely young men on super snazzy bikes in full professional team cycling kit appeared out of nowhere. They came whizzing past me heading in the same direction as me. They belonged to the professional cycling team Sunweb (changed to team DSM.) They might have been the junior academy or now I am so old that even the seniors look like juniors to me. I didn't care either way, they were human beings, and I was no longer alone. Even though they tore past me at supersonic speed they still found the time to encourage me to follow them by shouting "Allez! Allez!"

I loved seeing the young guns on their bikes. They were the epitome of health and fitness. They made cycling look so easy, and I was in awe of them. Not wasting any time, I jumped back on my saddle and did my absolute best to catch up with them. It was time to show the kids that even us older women can "do it!"

I hurled myself down the last hill and picked up a lot of momentum. Giving my legs one very big push I managed to get up the last little climb with relative ease. As I came over the summit I was delighted to see Team Sunweb were just ahead and had stopped at a crossroads for a chat. My bike freewheeled of its own accord and parked itself right in the middle of their meeting. All I could do was smile and say "Hola!"

It would seem that not only did the professional cyclists have incredible fitness, but they also had impeccable manners and kindness. (They must have a help-the-aged programme in their training regime!) They were so sweet and were very complimentary to me about my accomplishment of getting through the Valley of the Tears. They gushed that I was "Super Woman" and assured me that it was an extremely tough route even for them. They reiterated how impressed they were that a mere mortal like me would have the gumption to take it on and survive. While they never asked me my age they tactfully and politely asked me if I'd been cycling for long. While we were on the subject of time, I couldn't help but ask them how long the route had taken them from start to finish. Even though they had taken half the time it had taken me to complete I didn't mind at all. After all, they were half my age, 23 (I asked,) fine, fit, healthy young men who were all hoping to be on the pro tour in the coming season.

After a little chat and an obligatory selfie, the team said goodbye to me and jumped back on their bikes. I waved them off and enviously watched them as they whizzed off into the distance. They weren't in any way tired from the arduous route, in fact they looked like they were just starting out for the day. In comparison, I was wrecked and looked totally dishevelled but nevertheless, I had completed the exact same route as the professionals. I was jealous of their freshness but remembered at the same time that I was old enough to be their mother and they were also half my body weight! I slowly rolled out of the valley, to the small town of Ayacata, where I was extremely glad to find a typical Spanish bar serving cold drinks and food.

I thanked whoever was listening (in heaven) once again for getting me through another rollercoaster of emotions and out the other side of them to the finish, feeling happy and proud of my achievement. I especially thanked the bar owner profusely for the extra olives he gave me as he thought I looked a bit skinny. I took that compliment with gusto even though I knew that my pudgy little belly, which was happily hanging out over the top of my cycling shorts, had slowed me down a lot on the holiday.

Luke arrived in one piece too but like myself he had struggled through the valley. We got him some food, but unfortunately he didn't get much of a chance to rest as we had to chase the daylight in order to get home to the coast safely. It was such a tough day from start to finish but at the same time, it was very memorable, and I am glad that I did it. After all, nothing ventured, nothing gained.

Floating in the sea after such a tiring day was heaven. For the last time on the trip my body was lovingly kissed better by the waves. The water was wonderfully salty and pleasantly warm which soothed my soul and massaged my sore muscles. It had been a long day for sure, yet as I paddled in the sea watching another perfect sunset I forgot all about the pain and anguish I had endured that day and only remembered the highlights.

As I relaxed in the water I relived the wonderful moments from the trip. I was thrilled that I had taken the opportunity to travel when I could. I felt very grateful for all the fabulous dinners I had eaten outdoors by the sea. I was tanned and refreshed and even though I had gone a bit mad on my bike, I was glad that I managed to burn off all of the frustration and stress that I felt pre-departure.

When the sun dropped below the horizon and my last sunny day in Gran Canaria ended, I was overcome with tears. I really didn't want to go back home. There was a flood of mixed emotions going through my head. I wasn't ready to endure Christmas in Ireland or the darkness of the extremely short days in December. A knot started to form in my gut. I wasn't sure if it was from anxiety, dread, fear, panic, terror or a combination of them all.

In truth, I think those feelings in my gut were due to the sneaky suspicion I had of what was about to happen next. Unfortunately, I was right because a few days after I landed back in Dublin, the Irish government announced that Ireland was going back into a severe lockdown...

PORTUGAL & SPAIN

Chapter 20
I'm cycling through Spain, see you in Portugal!
Spain and Portugal 2021

My tan from Gran Canaria soon became a distant memory and by February I was pasty white yet again. Even though I was regularly cycling each week, I was becoming a bit of a slob!

Ireland's lockdown during the dark winter months was beyond cruel. While the government dressed it up and made it sound like "the right thing to do," my stress levels were rising tenfold each day and my anger at the world leaders and big pharma was off the Richter scale.

Physically, my bulging tummy that I had lugged around Gran Canaria had become a permanent fixture and my bed was seeing me for longer and longer each day. I was becoming institutionalised from sitting at home alone looking at the four walls and even talking to them at times. My lifelong hopes and dreams to travel far and wide were not enough to keep me going anymore. My smile was broken, and my spirit was most definitely crushed.

Mentally, I was really struggling. My tried and tested, failsafe solutions for hard times were not working for me. When I sat down to write in my journal I couldn't think of anything to "say." My head was like a barren waste ground with the odd tumbleweed rolling through it. I couldn't goal-set, no one could, as there was no sign of the harsh restrictions easing. Having nothing to look forward to was the hardest part of lockdown for me. I didn't have any travel plans in my diary, no sporting events to train for or social occasions to dress up for. It felt to me like I had been transported to hell and there was no way out.

Just to be sure that winter was the worst one ever, my mother was diagnosed with cancer. As you can imagine it was terribly upsetting news. It was such a shock as somehow, I never expected cancer to hit our family. I don't know why but I always had us down for heart attacks! However her diagnosis was very real and one that forced my family and myself to get our priorities right. Nothing else mattered and everything that was going on in the world was suddenly inconsequential to me. All I wanted was for my mother to get better.

Without any hesitation or time-wasting, she was taken into surgery. As you can imagine the situation took a major toll on my mother's health. We were sick with worry, but worst of all, we were completely helpless. Even though I would never class myself as religious, I was lighting candles and praying hard for good news as we waited for her results. After a very stressful three months, thankfully someone somewhere heard those prayers. Miraculously my mother got an "all clear" result. She was free to get on with her life. The whole family breathed a very big sigh of relief.

With that good news, and I guess having thought about my own mortality, I got a second wind for life and started to take better care of myself again. I didn't like looking at my jelly belly in the mirror and I certainly didn't like the way it jiggled from side to side when I walked! What would Jane Fonda think of me? I had to call on her for help. While she had been on a sabbatical for the last few months she was ready to kick ass into shape at a moment's notice. It took time to budge my bulge. It hadn't appeared overnight and was not going to just wash away but I persisted.

I set my alarm clock every day and as hard as it was to get up and get to my exercise mat, I was always glad that I did. I worked hard and lost inches thanks to a good weight training regime multiple times per week. The more I exercised the better I started to feel in myself. I also started to eat much better too. I had to. I knew deep down that my diet left a lot to be desired and the poor condition of my skin, hair and nails were hard to ignore.

During that time I was in touch via video calls with friends from all over the world that I had met while travelling. One evening while chatting to Monika in Madrid, my wonderful friend that I had made on the Lost City trek in Colombia, she could hear in my voice that I was not myself. She was worried about me and insisted that I visit her, immediately! She was excited to tell me that Madrid had reopened, we could go for meals, sightsee and hang out in the sunshine. It was music to my ears; life was out there, and I was going to be a part of it. Even my passport was shouting loudly with glee from the depths of the drawer it was buried in. I couldn't wait to book a trip to Spain and meet my friend again.

As luck would have it my sister was also due to have a milestone birthday later in the summer, August, and was having her "party" in Portugal. (Ireland was reopening for travel from mid-July so it was no problem). We, the family, were all expected to be there.

Don't ask me why or where I got the notion from, but I thought that it would be a great idea for me to cycle from Santander, on the very north coast of Spain, all the way down through the country to the south coast. Along the journey I would pop into Madrid for a few days, spend time with Monika and continue onwards. Once I got to the south coast, I planned to cycle west into Portugal and meet my family for a well-earned break, birthday celebrations and some long overdue fun.

My family all thought I was bonkers but at the same time they were so used to me, that they knew better than to try and stop me. I had never contemplated anything like that in the past but with the way the world was unfolding I wanted more than anything to escape and be alone in a place where I couldn't understand the repetitious conversations. I longed to cycle for days on end on the open road, in glorious sunshine, with a little luggage, a camera and my Snoopy travel teddy.

Thanks to the internet, time and buckets of excitement, meticulously I planned three wonderful weeks in Spain. I allowed for plenty of overnight stops in fascinating historical cities that I had never imagined visiting before. My visit to Monika and Madrid was in the middle of my adventure which gave me a good schedule to stick to. On paper I had it all worked out; I only booked the first few nights' accommodation in case I was running late or liked somewhere so much that I wanted to stay on. My big trip included Santander, Los Picos de Europa, (a mountain range in the north of Spain), Salamanca, Madrid, Seville and Cordoba.

I practised cycling with my luggage around Dublin. I had a back loader for my bike: it's a holdall bag that attaches to the saddle post and suspends from the underside of the seat. I had to make a few tweaks with industrial tape to make it fit perfectly on my small bike frame but otherwise it was perfect.

I also planned and pre populated each of my cycling routes onto my bike computer so there would be no chance of getting lost. Some days my cycles were short (60km) while my longest day was going to be 140km but flat as a pancake. As it was my first solo bike tour, I felt sure that I was organised and had all my ducks in a row. All I had to do was count down the days and practice my Spanish in earnest.

Unfortunately, just three weeks before my departure date I had a very bad accident on my commuter bike. I was cycling along minding my own business when out of the blue, WHAM! I hit a massive crater in the road and was thrown off my bike. I ended up splattered across the road, dazed and quite shaken.

Instantly I turned black and blue from deep bruises and was sore all over from hitting the rock-hard road. I was also covered in deep cuts, nicks and scratches. To top it all off my knee buckled beneath me when I tried to stand up. I was sure that my cruciate ligaments were badly damaged.

The two paramedics who came to my rescue were very nice men, cyclists too as it turned out. They were very sweet and chatty as we drove at speed to the hospital. They managed to distract me from the intense pain in my throbbing leg and my right hand which was skinned raw. For the second time during the pandemic I was being rushed to hospital with traumatic injuries from trying to be fit and healthy! It felt like I just couldn't win at all.

After five hours in Accident and Emergency I was released and hobbled out on crutches. Nothing was broken but due to severe inflammation they couldn't be entirely sure how my knee was. I needed to return after a few days for a second opinion. I was so upset, in fact heartbroken. I was totally deflated and felt like the whole world was against me. I sat on a bench outside St Vincent's hospital entrance while waiting for my brother-in-law to collect me and cried my eyes out from sheer despair. I felt like I was beaten. For all my good intentions and effort to look after my mental health it felt that, just like before, everything I touched was a disaster. I didn't know how I was going to get over the anguish I was feeling and I honestly wondered if I had the strength to get myself out of the "dumpster" once again.

Even after a good night's sleep, I still felt hopeless and fed up with absolutely everything. 2020 had been bad enough for all of us and even though it was only June, I was done with 2021.

After a few days, the swelling did go down and I went for my second check-up. The doctor felt that just by looking at my knee it was fine, but I still had my concerns considering how unstable it felt. (In hindsight, I am one hundred percent sure my kneecap was fractured as it took so long to heal. I couldn't put my full weight on it for around eight weeks and it was painful to straighten fully!)

Even though my hand was still raw and my knee was weak, there was no way I was cancelling the trip; if I had to pedal with one leg or go on a scooter I was going to make my tour happen.

I had done enough injury rehab in my time to know how it goes. Without any hesitation I took as many trips to the sea as I possibly could. Splashing around in the cold water I tried desperately to get my knee to cooperate. The rest of my body was glad of the water too; floating around, weightless and relaxed, my cuts and bruises soon became ripples in the water as my body recovered. At home

I was using ice packs, elevation and massage. I was even talking to my kneecap, willing it to get better with kind words. It made me feel better if nothing else. I found some holy water in a drawer someone had gifted me from the shrine of Knock and rubbed it on my knee twice daily for good measure too. If I had to, I would have sold my soul to the devil to get my knee fully operational and pain free.

Ten days later I went back to the Orthopaedic doctor for another check-up. Even though I expressed concern, he was very confident my knee was fine and encouraged me to go for a few short easy cycles and evaluate it for my impending trip. He was sure I would manage perfectly well on my bike but prescribed me some highly addictive painkillers just in case!

As tempted as I was to have a party on them and gobble the whole lot, I never went to the pharmacy and bought them. I wanted to; I really did. I felt like some mind-altering pain killers were exactly what I needed to get me through the pandemic. If the tablets reduced my knee pain, that would be a very helpful secondary bonus.

However, much to my frustration I had to be strong and boringly sensible. I was aware of myself all too well at that stage of my life. I just couldn't trust myself with prescription drugs given how down I was, especially with my tendency to take things to the extreme. Being in excruciating pain was definitely the lesser of the two evils! Bravely, I tore up my prescription and told myself I was great for doing so. (I didn't believe that for one second, I was just trying to make myself a martyr.)

As recommended by the "specialist" for my short, easy, test bike ride, I cycled from Dublin in the east to Castlebar in the west of Ireland in aid of charity. (245 kilometres!) I figured that would be as good a test as any. My knee was still bloody sore to walk on, but cycling was actually OK. There was a tiny bit of discomfort but nothing I couldn't manage. I was very happy with that result after all I was going to cycle the length of Spain, not walk it.

Even though technically we were not supposed to leave Ireland for another two weeks I didn't give a hoot. At 5am on the 6th of July 2021, once again as enthusiastically as my knee would allow, I hobbled into Dublin airport for departure to Spain. My bike was securely packed in a cardboard box, padded up with just the few clothes I was taking. The way I felt that day, I honestly didn't care if I never came back to Ireland. I had everything I needed, my bike, my passport, Snoopy and me.

I gave Ireland the one fingered salute as my plane climbed higher and higher in the sky to take me to the continent. Sunny Barcelona was my first port of call where I enjoyed a very relaxed bike tour around the magnificent city. The next day, I departed for the north coast. While the internal flight from Barcelona to Santander was short, unfortunately it turned into a nightmare. Not one piece of luggage made the flight. I arrived in Santander to find my bike and all my clothes were still in Barcelona. (Thankfully, I had my Snoopy travel teddy with me. It's funny, while I love to be alone, I still need a little something for comfort especially in times of stress.)

How could I start my cycling tour of Spain with no bike? The airline told me to "hang in there and buy yourself some deodorant!" They assured me they would deliver my bike to me in 48 hours' time. I was expected to just sit around and not make an issue out of it. What the actual f**k!

I was annoyed to say the least. I wondered what I was putting out into the universe to get so much crap flung at me? Was my karma really that bad?

My itinerary was immediately thrown into disarray. I had to urgently reschedule accommodation bookings, push everything back by two days and figure out where I could make up some lost time. I had to be in Madrid on set days as Monika was expecting me. There was no way I was going to miss seeing her: I would sacrifice the whole trip if I had to, to ensure our reunion went ahead.

The hardest part was just waiting around for my luggage to arrive. I felt powerless and had to learn some patience, not an easy thing for me. I just wanted to get going, hit the road and start my adventure. However it was not the worst disaster I had ever encountered when travelling so I did what I do best, sucked it up. Besides, there were worse places to be stranded than Santander. I used those two days to relax and give my knee a little more time in rehab. I took a very nice boat trip along the coast, ate lots of churros and sat in the sun. I also got to practise my Spanish in cafes and at my guest house. I was very pleased that I was able to make myself understood and change all my travel plans through speaking Spanish. I was especially thrilled that no one asked me to repeat myself which gave me a huge confidence boost regarding my ability to speak the language. All was not so bad after all.

Sure enough, after my 48-hour delay, the lady at the guesthouse reception shouted for me to come, I had a delivery. My cardboard bike box was standing in the hall, and I was over the moon to see it. All I had to do was assemble my bike and get going.

"The way I see it, if you want the rainbow,
you gotta put up with the rain."

-Dolly Parton.

Chapter 21
Sunflowers and the open road
Spain and Portugal 2021

I couldn't wait to get out my toolbox and roll up my sleeves. It took a little while and only one phone call to my very helpful friend Liam for some reassurance that I had built my bike correctly. After I double checked that all the screws were tight, I packed my clothes into my back loader and stuck it on the saddle post. My gorgeous "black beauty" bike and I were all set to hit the open road.

My first day was just sixty-five kilometres west to a fishing town, San Vicente de la Barquera. I planned to take the route at a leisurely pace with plenty of stops and photos along the coast. With the sun shining brightly and my fancy summer cycling kit on, I pressed start on my bike computer. My route navigation sprang into action, pointing me west for the official start of three weeks in Spain. Sitting comfortably on my saddle, I was more than excited and determined to have the ultimate trip of a lifetime. Myself and Snoopy departed Santander into the unknown.

My luggage back loader was a complete nightmare that day. I wondered how on earth I would cycle the length of Spain with it. I was travelling with the bare minimum: my luggage only weighed 2 kilos. Yet while I was riding my bike the bag was swinging all over the place and making balance a challenge. It even slipped down the saddle post and hit the back wheel bringing me to an abrupt stop. Gosh darn it! (I used more colourful words). I spent the most part of that short cycle trying to sort out my bag and make it stay still. I was so frustrated and ready to cry. My romantic notions of cycling on the open road with the sun in my face and touring Spain were turning out more like a road trip from hell.

After the tenth "bag stop," I ripped it off my bike and threw it on the road. In no uncertain terms I gave it a piece of my mind and even kicked it hard for good measure. It was really trying my patience and screwing up my amazing trip. I warned it if it didn't behave it was going to become a bonfire!

Using the very last of my industrial tape, I squished my bag tighter and made it even smaller and sturdier. I could just get my hand inside of the bag and poked my clothes to the very bottom. It worked! I didn't care what crumbled state my belongings were in, it's not like I was going to win any fashion awards anyway! Once again, I began my much needed adventure. Thankfully from that moment onwards my bag behaved itself. Hallelujah!

The North of Spain was full of medieval towns: I especially loved Santillana del Mar where I stopped and had a long lunch. It was a wonderful, cobbled stone town with rickety doorways and buildings that tilted slightly sideways. It was the perfect place for lunch plus it had lots of tourist shops selling local blue cheese and olives. While I didn't have room in my bag for any extra luggage, I had space in my stomach! I made sure to make the most of all the free cheese samples each shop had to offer.

After a tough start to my travels, eventually I arrived at San Vicente de la Barquera for the night. On the plus side, my knee had managed perfectly well on the bike for the day. While it was still a little sore to walk on, I enjoyed pottering around the busy fishing village. There was no shortage of restaurants serving their "catch of the day." The smell and extensive variety of seafood available was more than welcome to a tired and weary cyclist who had a hard first day. As it was summer, there were hordes of Spanish tourists milling around the small high street which gave the town a lively atmosphere. I loved everything about the village, it was a wonderful place to immerse myself into "real" Spain.

Setting off on day two of my journey, my destination was Los Picos de Europa, a mountain range in the north of Spain. The cycle was problem free and I finally felt as if I was a real adventurer like the ones I had seen on social media. Not to be outdone, I posted to my Instagram account stunning photos of myself, Snoopy and "Black Beauty" on our travels.

The Picos de Europa Mountain range was stunning and not something I expected to find in Spain at all. As you know every March I cycle all over the Sierra Nevada in the south, which is drier and dustier. The Picos were the complete opposite. The mountain range was lush with vegetation, alpine trees and gushing rivers. It was the very essence of fertility. The evenings were refreshingly cool too, making it easy to get a good night's sleep. I stayed in two wonderful towns, Los Arenas and Potes. Both were equally historic and pretty but best of all, there were plenty of excellent restaurants for a hungry cyclist to stuff her face with tasty local food.

While my trip was all about escapism there was no way I was going to miss a famous climb, the Covadonga, while I was in Spain. I had worked my itinerary around a few days in the Picos for that very reason. The Covadonga has been featured many times in the Vuelta, the professional cyclists' Tour of Spain. The pictures of the summit looked impressive, with two lakes at the top. Just like the Dolomites in Italy, there were rolling meadows, beige coloured cows and buttercups. To get there I needed to cycle through a national park and tackle a super steep section (that broke my heart!) My route was a hundred-kilometre round trip from the town of Las Arenas but thankfully I was luggage-free that day.

Needless to say, completing the Covadonga was hard. While the north of Spain was much cooler than the south, it was still very hot, 28 degrees. I was drenched with sweat and had to stop numerous times for water breaks. Even though I was cycling such a tough route I made the decision to take that iconic climb at a leisurely pace. After all, I had not gone to Spain to add any more hardship to my life. When I needed to stop for a break I did. I didn't even care how long it took me to get to the lakes because I had all day. Besides the viewpoints were spectacular; I could see all of northern Spain from them and once again I felt very small in the grand scheme of the universe.

The sky was bright blue, perfectly cloudless, giving a wonderful backdrop to the large hawks that were soaring high above me. They were unbelievably impressive: their expansive wingspan made them easy to follow as they flew in circles playing with the gentle warm winds. Mesmerized by their beauty I was happy to watch them for a while, catch my breath and soak up all the natural wonders I was grateful to witness. Before departing Ireland, I had not given any thought to what I would see on my trip. I was so overwhelmed at home that I just needed to get away and in all honesty really didn't care what I saw. Yet when I watched them gliding through the air, I was gently reminded that it's not the destination that matters, it's what you experience along the way that matters.

After every struggle comes a just reward. The lakes at the top of the Covadonga were out of this world. The first one, Lago Enol, was lovely. It was perfectly still and perfectly mirrored the mountains in the backdrop. While that was very scenic, I was more amused by the cows that were grazing peacefully in the sunshine. They didn't mind the traffic or tourists one bit. They sat on the side of the road oblivious to the most beautiful surroundings they were living in. Even though I had not reached the highest of the two lakes I very much enjoyed a much-needed rest and opportunity to take some photos.

To get to the very top, there was yet another steep drag which brought me up to the other lake, Lago Ercina. When I came around the last corner and entered the little car park, three bus drivers were leaning up against a wall. Chatting to each other while having a break, they looked relaxed as they soaked up the sun. Each of them had their shirt sleeves rolled up and were puffing on cigarettes while surrounded by the freshest of air. When they caught sight of me cycling slowly towards them, half dead on my bike, they quickly stood to attention, cheered and clapped while loudly shouting "Brava! Brava! Brava!"

218

I was extremely happy that someone acknowledged my tremendous struggle and pain to arrive there. I was smiling from ear to ear and trying to sit more upright! Even though I was wrecked they were super impressed by my athleticism. They even complimented my beauty which made me blush and simultaneously wonder about their eyesight given the state of me. Should they really be driving tourist buses? I was also delighted to converse with them in Spanish. I told them all about my arduous day and noted how difficult some parts of the route had been. They all nodded in agreement while continuing to smile, talk and smoke at the same time. Even though I was exhausted, ready to faint with hunger and struggled to find some words, my Spanish was comprehensible to them. For a fleeting moment I felt like a Latin Goddess!

I had to have a litre of water, an ice cream and a cold cola drink before I could do anything. My limbs were shaking from the effort, and I felt a little nauseous from the heat. My hair was soaking wet, and my cycling shorts were covered in white rings from all the salt I had perspired in my travels to get there. The surroundings were so beautiful that I sat in the field looking at the lake and mountains for an hour if not longer. I wished that my cycling friends were there with me to enjoy the views; they would have loved the scenery. In order to include them on my cycle I duly sent them a photograph of my vista and made them all mad with jealousy.

The rugged grey mountains wrapped around the landscape, framing the lake beautifully in my photos. There were even little bits of snow at the top when I looked closely enough. I loved the meadow, filled with buttercups and dandelions, where bumble bees and other insects were happily getting on with their busy life. It was such a lovely place to have a well-earned break before my return cycle. Later that day, when I got back to my guest house I was frazzled but at the same time I felt totally invigorated from being in nature for the day.

Sometimes a change of plan is required, not just in life. Part of my route wasn't going to work. My careful planning and itinerary schedule seemed perfect on paper but then when you're sitting in Ireland on a computer it's hard to know the reality of the roads.

219

To get out of the Picos mountains and start my three-day cycle to Salamanca I had to go up and over another arduous climb. It was twenty-three kilometres long; I would also have to do it with my luggage: the extra weight would slow me down no end and make the day very painful.

As you know I don't give up easily but after the Covadonga and the luggage debacle I just couldn't be arsed making life any harder for myself. For the first time ever, I arranged a taxi to drive me to the top of a climb! As we drove up the road and I saw how tough it would have been to cycle up it I was thrilled with my decision. I didn't even give a hoot what anyone would think about it either. I finally had reached the point in my life where I realised I had nothing to prove to anyone.Waving goodbye to my driver, I started my journey south with a huge downhill to the midlands of Spain which were flat as a pancake.

That day I got even more into my groove; it was exactly how I imagined my cycle would be. I felt like the bike was carrying me and every pedal stroke seemed to take me three times farther than usual. With the smooth roads and warmth of the sun my bike felt like a convertible Ferrari! Everything that day went according to plan. It was better than perfect. I stopped on bridges and took gorgeous photos of the lakes and rivers I passed. I was still in the north of Spain, where the landscape was wonderfully green.

As I was traveling so light there was a fair bit of laundry to take care of. I got into a little routine of arriving at my sleepover town by 2pm, thereabouts. I made sure the first thing I did was to have a huge lunch and then find my guest house. My one and only cycling kit got washed every single day in the shower with me. We had our little ritual of shampoo and rinse. I actually really enjoyed it, there was something relaxing about doing laundry by hand or in my case, with my feet. Each day I pretended I was crushing grapes as I stomped around the shower happily squeezing out my clothes while singing loudly to myself. Scrubbed up and dressed in one of my two changes of "normal" clothes I had the afternoon and evening free to hit downtown!

Wandering around whatever town or city I was in; the main objective of my excursion was to find the supermarket. Spain had the best selection of summer fruits, fresh off the trees, ripe and juicy, so I was in heaven. Every day I looked forward to my trip to the fruit section. It was a good way to learn my food vocabulary, but more than that, it was a festival of colour, shapes and sizes. The peaches were so large, the first time I saw them I mistook them for melons. The strawberries were so vibrantly red they looked like mini fire extinguishers! As for the apples, they were jumbo sized and so firm I could probably have stood on them if I needed to. Every day I bought two big bananas, two humongous peaches, and a litre of freshly squeezed orange juice that was super tangy and bursting with vitamins. Just for balance I also bought a big bag of salty crisps, purely for hydration purposes. I was so shocked by the price of fruit in Spain too, it was practically free. To be honest, it was just as well; my trip was not exactly being sponsored by a corporate logo. I was on a shoestring budget but was more than happy to make it work for me.

Some days I had to bring my newly washed cycling kit out for a walk with me. Often my bedroom didn't have a balcony or there was no direct sun to dry my gear. There were many times when I sat on a bench in the middle of a town square, licking an ice-cream with my wet cycling kit hanging off a chair beside me in the blistering sun. The locals never minded - it often gave them a chuckle to see my clothes drip drying and at times it made a good opening line for a conversation. The further south my trip took me the hotter it got. I went from having to use a hairdryer while in the north of Spain to get my shorts dry, to the south where it was so hot that I could not hang my cycling kit out to dry for any longer than ten minutes as the Lycra started to melt.

As much as I loved Spain, the one thing I could not get used to was the restaurant opening hours. They just opened and closed at the drop of a hat or at least that's how it felt, especially as I was hungry all the time. Very often in the evening when I was tired and ravenous I walked around towns trying to find a restaurant open for dinner. They'd all say the same thing, "come back later!" I just didn't get it, the staff were there, the lights were on, the doors were open but yet they were closed.

I was buying more and more in the supermarket each day to ensure I didn't starve to death, but I never really felt that I was full. I was burning calories for fun on my bike and rarely got to refuel each night. By the time the restaurants opened, it was so late in the evening I was zonked and ready for bed. As I was heading further south each day, the temperatures were soaring. It was the middle of July after all. I had to ensure that I was on my bike and on the road earlier and earlier with each passing day. Breakfast became my main meal, shortly followed by a decent elevenses. I always made sure to get a good lunch when I arrived in each destination. After that I survived on my supermarket fruit, ice cream and whatever I could find open at 6pm, which sometimes was nothing!

Cycling through the countryside was everything I imagined it to be. Waking up each morning I was greeted by clear blue skies, heat and unlimited time. Even though I tried to be in my next overnight destination by around 2pm each day, if it took longer or shorter I didn't mind at all. I had all day to tour and take as many detours as I wanted to. One day I found a wonderful cathedral in the city of Palencia. I was cycling along the river en route to the city of Valladolid when I spotted an incredibly large and ornate spire. The great thing about travelling on my own was that in the blink of an eye, I stuck out my hand and indicated to change direction. I am so glad I did as I found the most spectacular paved concourse with a huge Gothic cathedral soaring towards the heavens. It was a truly spectacular feat of engineering. As much as the building fascinated me, I spotted something that was even more interesting and beautiful.

Large white storks had built their nest between the two spires, and they were so high up I had to crank my neck to see them clearly. The storks ironically had a bird's eye view of the entire city and their newest fan. They were clearly very happy in their penthouse suite with a postcode that money could not buy. I loved the huge storks in Spain so much. Everywhere I went I easily spotted their mammoth sized nests that were delicately built in the most precarious of places. Most of the time the nests were occupied with two birds, who sat looking out while watching the world go by. I cycled past a very large statue one day and wondered why he had a great big hat on his head. When my eyes focused clearly it was another bumper sized nest with my beloved white storks peering out from behind their amazing natural feat of engineering. They made me chuckle every time I saw them. They had no shame in where they built their homes. Every city I went to on my trip I checked out the churches and cathedrals, not just for the history but more importantly to see the storks who had commandeered the spires.

The roads were peaceful too, free not just from traffic but from the constant bombardment of the media and other people. I had officially unplugged from life and was more than content on my own. I adored the long flat stretches of open road that I cycled on for miles and miles. I loved how strong and fit I was feeling. and just like when I was in Cuba, and Gran Canaria, I had some great tunes playing loudly in my back pocket. I love 90s dance music and ensured I had a good old sing song most days. It was pure bliss; I was outdoors in nature and was enthralled with scenery especially when I saw acres and acres of yellow fields.

At first I thought they were rapeseed plantations, the same as we have in Ireland, but I was very wrong. They were fields of dreams, magical and straight out of a fairy-tale. They were sunflower fields. Thousands upon thousands of large yellow heads stood to attention as I cycled by.

Pulling in to take pictures I did my best to do the magnificent fields justice but in the end I decided that some things cannot be photographed with a camera. It was better to lodge the picture in my head instead. I memorised the view and the smell, but most of all I tried to remember the moment, the feeling of happiness and joy so that I could recall it another time. Each and every flower was uniquely perfect. Their wonderful heads, great big discs filled with tiny flowers, were intricately detailed up close. It was like looking into an entire solar system which hypnotised me with its delicate beauty. I felt blessed and honoured to spend time in the endless sunflower fields which were more brilliant and sunnier than the very sun that prompted them to grow.

I never tired of seeing the sunflowers. For three solid days I cycled alongside yellow fields, packed with sunny, happy heads. It felt as though sunshine was radiating out of them and fuelling me with enthusiasm and hope. It was my very own Yellow Brick Road taking me to a place where dreams do come true.

While I loved being in nature, some days I got a little more than I bargained for. On three separate occasions my route navigation got me into big trouble. The problem with online maps is when you plan a route for a bicycle it is assumed that your bike can go through any terrain. By that I mean rocks, sand, dirt roads and fields. No! My bike most certainly cannot plough through any old muck. It is a top of the range road bike, therefore it only likes to be on a properly sealed road with smooth tarmac. Road bikes are a little precious, you have to mind them and take special care of where you go on them. They don't like to get dirty; they are a bit like a fine stallion! They look the business, enjoy prancing around, live in clean stables and have a noble air of exquisiteness about them. Road bikes are not mules! If you want to go off road then you need a donkey. A good sturdy no-frills, industrial frame that will go for days and loves to get dirty. My poor bike did not like it when my route planning took us down dirt roads. Every time I took out my phone to double check the map, the route assured me the bad road would not be for much longer and a "real" road was ahead soon. Except it wasn't.

Once I cycled for over ten kilometres on a makeshift road through fields and farm backyards. It was so bumpy, my backside was sore, but I was more terrified that I would get a puncture. I was in the middle of nowhere and had no idea where the next town was. Sure, I can fix punctures, but it takes me all day. It's not that easy, I can get the tyre off but putting it back on is beyond painful. Another time my route took me down a farm lane and into the middle of a field. According to the online map I would reach a road at the far end of the field, but I didn't. Instead there was a large trench filled with swamp water and bugs. I had to double back that day, so instead of cycling one hundred kilometres I ended up cycling one hundred and forty. By the end of that day I was parched and scorched as well as extremely pissed off to say the least. To top that off, both my phone and power bank died as I was online for so long.

The third and last route disaster once again brought me down a sandy road. If I had a BMX bike it would have been great fun but not on my beautiful carbon princess! I really needed to get out of that desert. Not only was the sand way too thick to cycle on, but more seriously, it was no good for road bike components. I ended up having to walk through it while carrying my bike and luggage. I was the mule! The route had been perfect until I took a right turn and then had no clue where I was. After about forty minutes of walking through my very own Sahara Desert I spotted a road ahead, a real one, with black tarmac. Even though it was up on top of a very high bank I was adamant that I was going to get onto that road, and I didn't give two hoots where it went.

Climbing up a steep ditch in cycling shoes while dragging my bike with luggage was not how I pictured my touring trip of a lifetime. I was cursing my route planning. The map I was using clearly showed roads; it just didn't say that they were made of sand. Nobody posts reality on Instagram, people there all look so perfect, smug and clean. I wondered was it just me that these things happened to or was it that everyone else was just faking their trips?

My legs and arms got scratched to bits from the brambles in the ditch, and small dots of blood formed on my skin which I sucked off! Being a farmer's daughter I was not in the slightest bit concerned about bacteria. I grew up on a natural spring, spent my youth running around fields and ate sandwiches with dirty hands. I was sure I would live. My legs were bashed to bits too from the pedals knocking off my shins as I hauled the bike up the ravine. I was also completely out of water and dehydrated from the blistering sunshine. I was drenched in sweat, and the sand and muck from the ditch stuck to me, making me look like I had just climbed out of a swamp! The last push was difficult because my bike was tangled in the undergrowth. When I reached the top of the ditch, my feet were delighted to be back on tarmac; I just needed to free my bike from the scrub, pull it up a few more feet onto the road. I squatted as low as I could go and pulled with all my might to dislodge it. Not knowing my own strength the bike flew in the air towards me and knocked me flat on my back. Yet again, for the second time in a matter of weeks I lay splattered across a road! (This whole cycle touring thing was not easy by any means.) Dusting myself and bike off, I sat on the bank and had a cry. I really needed a pep talk and a hug to dissolve my self-pity. I also needed to find a new route to my destination. I caught myself saying "I am too old for this shit!"

When I heard those words fall out of my mouth I paused. Did I really think that or was it just a shitty day? I had to think about it for a few moments but deep down I knew the answer. It was just another detour, it was not exactly the end of the world. So what if my bike computer had brought me on a road that didn't actually exist, no big deal. God knows I have taken more than a few wrong turns in my life and yet somehow I have always got back on course. I looked at the positives of the situation, I was on a proper road and I could go forth and complete my mission. All was not lost, shit happens! It really does, I know that. There was no way I was going to write off my adventure and quit. I followed the road to a small town, got more water and had a cold soda. Sitting in the shade I was able to find a new route on my phone and get going once again.

Even with all my teething problems on the trip, I arrived on schedule into Madrid. I had made up for the lost two days by shaving off a sight seeing day in Salamanca and instead of cycling from there to Madrid, I took a lovely air conditioned train and escaped the blistering heat for three hours. While it was a pity in a way to have to speed up the journey, I was more than glad I did.

It was so wonderful to see Monika again and catch up on all the gossip from the last few years. We had stayed connected via the internet but there was no comparison with being together face to face. We picked up exactly where we left off, because even though we only travelled together for a short while in Colombia we had become friends for life. Excitedly we reminisced about Colombia and chatted about life in general, before we got to the real nitty gritty: men we had dated and cats. Two topics very dear to both our hearts. Catching up with her and having new conversations was refreshing and just the tonic I needed. We were both solo travellers when we first met and as it turned out, we were both still more than comfortable to be solo in our relationship status too.

During the daytime, while she was at work, I busied myself sightseeing in Madrid at my own pace. As you know the only way for me to see a city is on a cycling tour. I gladly swapped my carbon road for a sturdy city bike with a basket for a day. While it was heavy, it was perfect for getting around a busy urban area with potholes. I was joined by four funny and youthful people from Dubai who had come to Spain to escape the heat of the Middle East! It was hilarious, they were wearing jeans and remarking how pleasant the weather was while I felt like I had walked into a furnace. We had a good laugh on the tour though, as our guide was bubbly and friendly too. It was wonderful to meet new people and hear all about life in Dubai and learn about Madrid from a local.

I was also glad to take a break from the open road, use a washing machine for my kit and be in one place for three whole days. It felt like a mini break within a holiday. I loved Madrid even though visiting the city in July was just plain bonkers due to the heat.

Monika and I had wonderful meals out in the city. She brought me around her locality, and I got to see a snapshot of her life. I also met her friends and had good fun. I was thrilled that I had made visiting her the focal point of my tour. Monika was right, Madrid was "open", and life had resumed there. The streets were heaving with people of all ages enjoying meals al fresco. The city was alive, and I loved it. Only for the heat, I would never have left!

The three days flew by in a flash, and it was time to get back on my journey to the south of Spain. I was sad to say goodbye to Monika, but I know that we will see each other again, somewhere in the world. In the meantime, I was headed for the south coast, where the beaches and sea breezes were awaiting my big arrival.

I was on the road again, except it was in an airconditioned coach! I had been due to cycle through the dust bowl of southern inland Spain for two days from Madrid to Cordoba. However Monika assured me that there was nothing there and I would be better off skipping it. She advised me instead, to take extra days on the beach. Plus she warned me the temperatures were due to hit 44 degrees and it just was not worth the effort. I didn't need to think twice about her advice and once again on the trip, I decided to avoid inflicting pain on myself. With the help of a very nice bus, I was in Cordoba after just five hours. For an extra €10 I was able to bring my bike onboard too. It was a no brainer and a bargain. As the coach drove through the desolate midlands, I texted Monika to thank her for her advice and tell her she was right. I also took out my itinerary and for the second time on my trip, changed my plans.

Cordoba was my favourite city on the journey, even though it was boiling hot. The Alhambra (palace) opened at 7am for visitors and I made sure I was there at 6:55am. According to my phone weather app, it was 39 degrees at that hour of the day. I managed to sightsee until 11am, but after that I had to siesta for most of the afternoon as it hit 42 degrees. In the evening when it was a mere 36 degrees I wandered around the souvenir shops and small narrow, winding streets of the Moorish city. I really wanted to buy some mosaic tiles which Andalucía is famous for, they were so colourful and bright. However I still had a long way to go on my bike to reach my family in Portugal. I didn't dare try to fit anything else into my luggage bag and ruin my run of good luck. (I will just have to go back another time and shop to my heart's content).

From Cordoba I cycled 130 kilometres southwest to Seville. I had to leave at the crack of dawn to try and beat the heat, but who was I kidding? There was no escaping it. Mind you, when I was on the bike I didn't mind the hot air so much as I was moving through it. I found it quite pleasant to be honest, plus my mind was occupied with route navigation, playing music and basking in my freedom. It was only when I stopped for refreshments that I was instantly dripping wet. Sweat rapidly formed puddles under me as I queued in shops to pay for gallons of liquids. On the positive side it was so hot that I didn't feel like eating at all and was looking a lot slimmer for it. I was practically living on just cold liquids by that stage of my trip. My tan was coming along nicely too and at times I was mistaken for a Spaniard. That was until I opened my mouth. While my Spanish was improving there was no denying by my accent that I was not from around those parts.

My cycling odyssey continued from Seville to the south where I finally hit the coast. When I caught my first glimpse of the sea I was so overjoyed that tears automatically streamed down my face.

I had made it, and even though I had taken an unexpected lift in a taxi, a train and coach, I was immensely proud of myself. It hadn't been easy but overall I loved every minute of the journey. It felt like a lifetime ago that I had started in Santander on the north coast even though it was only two and a half weeks. So much had happened in that time, I had seen so many beautiful places and met my dear friend. While I loved my trip through the centre of Spain I was beyond relieved to be on the coast. I am drawn to water and feel much happier when I know the coast is nearby. (I think deep down in my subconscious I am always looking for an escape route). I won't be moving to landlocked Nepal any time soon, that's for sure.

I could not wait to jump into the sea and splash around like a child. While I am no mermaid, I just love how being in the water feels so liberating. My extra days that I had banked thanks to the bus were very well spent. I lay on the beach, snoozed in the sun, frolicked in the sea and ate copious amounts of ice cream. It was pure bliss. Even though there were hordes of Spanish families running riot on the beach I was unaffected by them and in my own little slice of paradise. As I watched the waves rolling in and out on the shore, there was no doubt in my mind that my solo bike touring expedition and all the time I had spent outdoors had done me the world of good. I reminisced back to the time in my life when I didn't know the meaning of self-love and self-worth and thought people who talked about them were bonkers. Yet there I was completely content, bursting with inner joy, feeling proud of myself and dare I say it, having love for myself. Once upon a time I was my own worst enemy, but after everything I had been through over the years I had come full circle. Through thick and thin I was always there for myself, talking myself out of trouble and finding silver linings whenever the going got tough. I had shown myself a lot of kindness on the trip by taking short cuts on public transport and avoiding unnecessary hardship. Before I would have slogged it out and been a martyr. It was on that beach that I realised that I had reached "personal development enlightenment!" I was well and truly my own best friend.

With my newfound insight, I made some very important promises to myself while there. One was that I would not give up hope, there was always a solution if I just looked at life from a different perspective (or place!) I had let the winter and "rules" get on top of me and it felt at times that life was an endurance test. I had to find a way of dealing with those kinds of emotions if for any reason I could not travel.

I also promised myself to stop stressing about what I couldn't control. I didn't have to like those things or agree with them, but I had to learn acceptance (or find a loophole!) While acceptance would be extremely hard for me, especially about things that I feel are unjust and I am enthusiastic about, being stressed was not helping any situation in any way. I needed to find more productive and beneficial ways to fight for and uphold my values. That might mean biting my tongue, choosing my battles, having patience or walking away from situations. (Again very hard for me to do!)

Lastly, I decided that more down days were needed when I returned home. I loved it when I had taken valuable time to relax in Cuba and more recently enjoyed sitting on the coach rather than cycling in the heat. I needed to continue showing myself kindness and being more sensible. (There would be no more cycling mountains when severely sick or teaching classes with a snapped Achilles tendon either.)

While I was relaxing in Spain, my family was enroute to Portugal. I couldn't wait to see them all, celebrate my sister's special birthday and show off my amazing tan. I was mahogany, but with my two big blue eyes I looked a little odd. Most of all I couldn't wait to mess around on the beach with my niece and nephews in the sunshine.

After two rest days on the beach I started my journey west to the border between Spain and Portugal. I cycled along the coast to the Spanish port town of Ayamonte which was really quaint and welcoming. I celebrated the end of my splendid tour through Spain with a huge plate of Paella. I even allowed myself the purchase of a new straw hat for my impending week in Portugal. My bag was still tiny, and industrial taped within an inch of its life, but I was sure I could squeeze a straw hat in there for the last leg. Failing that I would wear it under my helmet if I had to.

I loved my time in Spain and having been to some outposts off the beaten track I was mesmerised by their culture and way of life. I had passed through so many beautiful cities, and in one fell swoop they were now all ticked off my bucket list. Santander, Salamanca, Madrid, Cordoba and Seville were all very interesting and wonderful to visit; however I was most definitely "cultured out." I had overdosed on cathedrals and palaces; I couldn't recall which monument was where and needed time out to organise the travel filing cabinet in my head.

On Thursday 29th July 2021, I cycled one kilometre from my hotel to the port of Ayamonte and bought my ferry ticket. It was €1.50 for me and €1.90 for my bike. Bargain! Rolling up the gangplank there were just four other passengers aboard the tiny vessel. The captain gave the horn a toot and we departed the dock. Black Beauty, Snoopy and I set sail for Portugal...

Chapter 22
Breakdown Assistance
Portugal 2021

It took just 12 minutes to cross the Rio Guadiana from Spain to Portugal. Chugging across the river I could see both countries during the entire cruise as they were so close. We were hardly out of the port in Spain and already the crew were getting ready to berth in Portugal. Excitedly, I sent my family a video of me and Snoopy on the boat. They could expect us to arrive in just a few hours' time. I was really looking forward to enjoying time with my family, packing my bike away and spending quality time horizontal on a sun lounger.

Once we docked, I rolled my bike down the gangplank and officially arrived in another country. Their green and red flag was waving proudly in the gentle breeze and there was a huge sign saying "Portugal." I was definitely in the right place.

I turned my clock back an hour to get onto Portuguese time and saddled up for one last jaunt. I was ready to give my bike a good lash for the last time before our well-deserved rest. My final cycle of the trip was just eighty-two kilometres from the port of Vila Real de Santo António to Villamoura. The quickest way to get there was up over the hills, through the town of Loulé. While it wasn't the easiest route, it would be worth the effort so that I could join in with the madness of my family on tour!

Enjoying the day and the new country, I pedalled away. Slowly at times so that I could admire the views. I was happily chatting and singing away to myself and any birds I saw. After the hills there was a very pleasant downhill and a refreshing breeze in my hair. I was cycling along thinking about what I might have for dinner with my family. There are a few restaurants that they like to go to, and I wondered which one would be that night's choice. I wouldn't have any say in it, I would just go along with their choice. After all, it was my sister's week so whatever she wanted, she could have.

It was an idyllic day and a wonderful route to finish my tour on. I was feeling very happy in myself and was thinking how great overall the trip had been. With no more than 20 kilometres to go I was whizzing along and counting down the kilometres to my big arrival. Suddenly, without warning there was a mighty BANG! I got the fright of my life. It was so dramatic, it's a wonder I didn't have a heart attack.

Instantly my bike started to wobble all over the place and was out of control. Luckily, I managed to get both of my feet onto the tarmac before I completely lost my balance. My back tyre had exploded. The side wall had burst wide open. It must have split due to the heat: most likely the inner tube must have expanded too much and caused the explosion! Gosh darn it, (insert colourful language here) I had gone all that way with no bike mechanicals, I couldn't believe it. With less than one hour left to my home I was up shit creek! I had a spare tube and tools but not a spare tyre.

Like any good damsel in distress I desperately tried to flag down a vehicle to help me. I had looked at the map on my phone: the next town, Loulé, was just five kilometres away, there were two decent bike shops in the town. I just needed a lift to one of those shops where I could sort my wheel out and get back on the road in no time. Unfortunately, thumbing a lift in Portugal was impossible. No one stopped for me. They saw me waving at them and proceeded to drive straight past me. I did get a few beeps which were of absolutely no use to me. In return they got a middle finger salute which I felt was more than a fair response.

Standing in the sun with a broken bike does not do a whole lot for your morale. I was so annoyed; they were brand new tyres and had only done 1,200 kilometres. I would expect to get double that out of an expensive tyre. However I had been off-piste a few times and it was ridiculously hot for the entire trip, so I suppose it wasn't surprising that they gave up the ghost. I could have picked up the phone and rang my dad to come and rescue me but that was the last thing I wanted to do. For the entire trip I had imagined our big family reunion. I had visions of me cycling to the gate of the complex where they would be waiting with bated breath. They would cheer and jump up and down with glee when they spotted me pedalling in on my final approach. There would be a massive group hug, kisses and even a balloon! There was no way in hell I was going to rock up in the back of a car with my pride in my shoes. Not only that, but my family are also a tough crowd, I would never hear the end of it. I would be reminded of my failed journey for eternity. I absolutely had to get to Villamoura on two wheels. Weighing up my options, I could have walked beside the bike and rolled it slowly to avoid damaging the wheel or as I had before in the sand, I could once again carry my bike 5 kilometres to Loulé.

Luckily, I didn't have to either because my guardian angel sent a hero my way! To be exact, he was a young and very handsome hero in cycling gear that came to my rescue on a very snazzy bike. He was half Portuguese and half Canadian, spoke perfect English and was more than willing to help me. He was such a polite young man. I asked him if he would mind flagging down a van and explaining to them, in Portuguese, that I needed a lift to the bike shop. He willingly obliged.

Would you believe it, not once but twice he managed to get a driver to stop for a chat. I was so impressed with his hitching skill but unfortunately both times the driver refused in no uncertain terms to help us. Seriously, they flat out said no and drove off at speed. I couldn't understand the mentality, they were going that direction. What was their problem? They had great big vans too with lots of room, my bike and I would have fitted in no bother, yet they were having none of it. We didn't get a reason from either driver, but it didn't matter either way. A flat out no is a no and that's all there was to it. My poor hero apologised profusely for his compatriots. He said it was typical of the Portuguese; according to him they are not helpful people. I didn't agree. After all, he had stopped to help me, so he had broken that stereotype in one go.

My wonderful hero said there was only one way to solve the problem. He was going to cycle to the town and go to the bike shop for me. He would purchase all the supplies I needed then cycle all the way back to me and be a hero, forever in my memory!

What a guy! He stuck to his word. I was a little worried when he cycled off with €50 belonging to me in his pocket, but I really had no other choice than to trust him. Besides, there are good people on this earth, and I knew instantly when I met him that he had a kind soul and a big heart. He wouldn't have stopped and offered to help me if he didn't want to. He was my own roadside rescue service with no annual subscription.

While he was gone I busied myself preparing the wheel for his return. Standing on the side of the road in a tiny scrap of shade, I had my bike turned upside down with the rear wheel off. Even with my tools all over the place and my luggage bag slung on the ground not one person in their vehicle stopped to check if I was ok. I wanted to scream my head off at the locals as more and more cars whizzed past me. I wondered to myself if once again I was being unreasonable expecting people to stop and help me. I know I would have, but then we are all different and that's life. I love that we are all unique and there are cultural differences but at the same time manners are free. Surely we all know that when you see a person in difficulty you help. Admittedly I was not drowning or bleeding to death, but every situation has its own complications. Were all the drivers really so busy that they could not stop for a minute...?

True to his word my young cycling hero came back with my shopping and even some change. He really was a knight in shining cycling gear. Not only that, but when he arrived back he jumped off his bike and proceeded to put the new tyre on for me. Swoon!

I really wished he were about 20 years older; he was certainly the most perfect man I had met in a very long time. Unfortunately, I was old enough to be his mother but if I were his mum, I would have been very proud of the fine, polite and helpful person he was.

Waving goodbye and thanking him profusely he went on about his business. Watching him cycle off into the sun I was thanking everyone and anyone in heaven and earth for sending me such a wonderful helper.

After a short food and beverage stop in Loulé as well as a bicycle pump stop in one of the bike shops, I was ready for the last leg of my trip. I gave the final twenty kilometres all that I had. I went full gas and burnt every last ounce of energy I had to get to our home from home. Turning into Vilamoura I knew exactly where I was. The old familiar roads and buildings that I had not seen in two years were still there, nothing had changed, and I was glad. I pulled in for just a second and sent my family a text message to say I was just three kilometres away. In other words, it was time to roll out the red carpet, strike up the band and ensure the town mayor was at the ready with a laurel wreath and yellow jersey for their local pro cyclist.

Whizzing around the numerous consecutive roundabouts, I was cornering them like a pro. My excitement and the gentle tail wind combined gave me a turbo thrust sending me into ludicrous speed. I was buzzing to be near the end of the trip and see everyone. I was sure that they were just as excited to see me too.

Around one last roundabout, I approached at speed, navigated the arc and took the final exit. Cycling up the last straight road, the gate to our complex was just 400 metres away. Lifting my head for a split second I could see the road was completely clear. For a fleeting moment I noticed the perfectly manicured grass either side of me. Down with my head, bracing my tummy muscles and pushing my little legs with all my might I tore up the road leaving a plume of smoke behind me! I had to squeeze so hard on my brakes to bring my bike to an abrupt halt that there was a smell of burning rubber.

I had arrived. Yippee! Panting and gasping for air I wondered where the welcoming committee was. No one was there. The gates were firmly shut.

Deflated, I stood at the perimeter wall and buzzed reception to let me in. They clearly had not been informed of the VIP arrival either as they just told me to push the gate open and come on in. I wondered if my family were going to surprise me and jump out from behind the wall with streamers and balloons.

Nope. Walking precariously over the cobbles with wobbly legs and cycling shoes while pushing my bike into a fancy resort was not how I had imagined my grand finale. I thought my family would be there to take my bike from me. I even thought they would help me and my jelly legs by making a sedan chair for me with their arms while simultaneously crowning me Ms Bike-World 2021 and draping a sash over my head. My heart was just a little in my boots especially when I spotted them all sitting under great big parasols enjoying their lunch and cocktails.

Perhaps they had missed the text I sent them a little while ago? When they eventually spotted me they did look up and give me a big whoop and holler. The other patrons in the establishment were duly alerted to the commotion even though they had no idea what was going on. My mum got up, ran over and planted a great big kiss on me. She was smiling ear to ear and said she was thrilled to see me. I know she worries when I go off on my adventures, but I am so good at keeping in touch. I phoned her daily and often at times during the trip I had brought her on a virtual tour of a church via a video chat. I didn't even charge her a tour guide fee! Other people in the complex that knew me came over and congratulated me on my achievement too. At last, a little fuss was made of me, and it gave me a warm fuzzy feeling.

Leaning my bike up against a parasol, people started to notice my lack of luggage. They struggled to believe me that the small beat-up bag covered in silver industrial tape was it. That's all I had with me for my trip through Spain. Thankfully my parents had brought some clothes to Portugal for me so that I could look all girly again and not like a homeless cyclist!

Guzzling a pint of fresh orange juice I was relaxed and unbelievably happy to be in Portugal with the gang. It felt right after
being alone for so long. I wanted to be with my family and as noisy
as they are when they are together, I was happy to be there in the
middle of the chaos. I was also more than ready to wear a bikini for
a week and do next to nothing.

The party for my sister's special birthday started the next day
as more friends and family arrived and fun was had by all. My adult
nephews and I decided that we needed a very memorable moment
to finish off such a monumental family gathering. They too had
missed birthdays and special occasions due to various lockdowns
and restrictions during the eighteen months and wanted to mark
the occasion.

The day before our departure back to Ireland myself and my
three nephews took a flight to 15,000 feet above sea level and sky-
dived back to earth. Jumping out of a perfectly good plane strapped
to a man is not the most logical thing in the world to do but it was
exhilarating. While my heart stopped for the first few seconds of
the jump, once it rebooted itself and kicked back into action I loved
skydiving. (Naturally, Snoopy was tucked into my boiler suit and
came for the jump too!) When the parachute opened, it felt like
time slowed down completely. I was floating along, high above the
Algarve coastline, observing how beautiful the world was and thanking my lucky stars that I was there, in that moment, alive and well.
I breathed a deep sigh of relief and let the warm air circle around
me as we gently drifted back to earth. I sure had come a long way,
not just on the map or in my atlas. Even though my nephews are all
men now, tall ones at that, it was the first time in a very long time
that we had got to spend quality time together. Ticking off a bucket
list experience with them was for me, the most fantastic memory
of the entire trip.

My tandem instructor and I landed with a bit of a thud but
either way it was perfect, we were down and alive! Rolling around
on the grass I was laughing so hard; I was high on adrenaline and
life. My nephews came dashing over to me, whooping and hollering with joy. We had a great big group hug and then proceeded to

jump around with glee. We were like four giddy goats who couldn't control themselves.

My month-long adventure ended on such a high, literally. I was glad that I had spent a lot of time on my own in Spain. I had cleared my head and reset my soul. Being with my niece and nephews for a few days was just the tonic I needed to invigorate me. They were a good reminder to stay young at heart, and on their side they appreciated having a fearless aunt who showed them an alternative lifestyle and a new route to Portugal.

Flying home to Ireland, I spent the journey writing a gratitude list of all the amazing places and things I had seen and done. The list was so extensive I ran out of paper and had to ask for napkins to write on.

That trip was badly needed, more than I can express. I am under no illusions how lucky I was to be able to take extended time out from life. I am just glad I did. It rejuvenated my own passion for life, made me forget about gloomy news bulletins and the mental overload I had been under. I knew I was not the only person who has struggled financially and mentally through the pandemic. I just was one of the lucky ones who had the chance to walk away, escape for a while and switch off from it.

Not only was my life waiting for me upon my arrival home, but there was also a kitten who needed a forever home. She had been found all alone, under a hedge, and was far too young to be without her mother. Knowing I was a sucker for animals, the person who found her sent me a photo and hinted that I could rescue her. The poor little thing was in a very sorry state. Even though she was tiny, dishevelled, skinny and a little unusual looking, she had an undeniable twinkle in her bright blue eyes. I just knew the instant I saw her picture that she was full of sass, gumption and determination. She was small and mighty too. We were definitely meant to be together.

When I met her, Sooty, my world changed in an instant. She needed a mother, love and playtime. Lots of playtime in fact. For the first time in my life, something was totally dependent on me. My world no longer revolved around me, myself and I. Was I sorry?

Not in the slightest. I was more than happy to give my time and love to her. She was the most adorable little thing in the world.

Having a pet to mind brought me to a whole new emotional level. While I had been in love before with humans, this was different. She was my "baby." While you might tell me to "shut up" and remind me that she is a cat and not a human, I don't care. She brought out a maternal side in me that I never honestly thought I had. I was besotted and welcomed her into my life with open arms and an open heart. I couldn't believe how much I loved her and enjoyed spending time on the floor playing games with her. Nothing else mattered in those moments.

Spending time at home alone was no longer a problem for my head. Instead of the walls closing in on me, my home expanded with all the feel-good hormones, cuteness and fun she brought to our home.

Being a cat, she did whatever she wanted when she wanted which made me love her even more. She didn't care if she walked over me while I was fast asleep or if she sat on my laptop while I was trying to write. She was so sassy and immediately took full ownership of my apartment, and me!

Some people told me I was crazy to take on a pet. Apparently it was "too much" for me and my lifestyle. They warned me that I wouldn't be able to drop everything and go travelling the way I was used to.

While they were right about not being able to travel on a whim, I didn't care in the slightest. I just had to plan my trips a little more than before and include "childcare" in my budget. It was no big deal. Besides, life is ever evolving, and she was more than worth it to have so much joy in my home.

As you probably guessed, my cat doesn't have a normal life. How could she when living with me? I bought Sooty a backpack and started having adventures of a different kind with my fluffy, four-legged friend!

Together, we are living our best life.

"You've always had the
power my dear,
you just had to learn it for
yourself."

-*Glenda, The Wizard of Oz*

Chapter 23
MY MESS IS MY MESSAGE TO YOU

Even in hindsight, I would not change any of my outlandish adventures. Not one moment. Not even the tears, tantrums, trials, and tribulations that I experienced along the way. They have all made me who I am today. While some might think that I am a little crazy I take it as a compliment. If they knew where I had been and where I am now they might prefer to call me resilient and admire my strength of character instead.

At the end of the day, your life boils down to one thing, how you feel about yourself. Having the gumption to spend time alone and find out what you are made of, be different or stand out from the crowd might be a little daunting at first, but trust me, you will get the hang of it in no time at all! As you can see from my stories, it is possible to be happy alone, have fun, travel and live your life your way.

I hope that I have encouraged and inspired you to fill your life with experiences, passions and fun as well as finding time to learn and grow personally. It's never too late to let your inner butterfly lose on the world. Fly and show off your amazing individual colours. You could of course stay wrapped like a caterpillar in a cocoon where it's dark and safe, but the sun doesn't shine in there!

If only I had known that back in 2005 when I felt lost and alone. Things would have been very different. I'm sure of it but as we all know, hindsight is a wonderful thing!

I would love to walk into that God-forsaken garden where the weeds couldn't be bothered to grow and sit on the bench beside the girl I once was. I would tell her everything that I have learnt over the years, especially how great her story turns out to be. I would let her know that unexpectedly, she is in fact the hero in her story. The one who turned it all around through her unwavering strength of character, tenacity and determination. I would tell her that she is enough, perfectly imperfect, already complete and has always been. She never needed to search for wholeness, especially not through relationships or by trying to fit in. I would love to tell her that all she ever needed was to drown out the noise and listen to her heart to find her own way.

I wonder if she would be happy to know that ultimately she would end up helping others who feel just as miserable as she was. That by going it alone, travelling solo, having courage and gumption she got the "mess" in her head under control. Lastly, I would put my arm around her and whisper in her ear, that she is loved and never, ever needs to feel so lost or alone again. Nobody does.

What would you tell your younger self?

My biggest insight is that being alone, single, (whether young or old) being different from the crowd or choosing to change direction isn't so scary after all. In fact it is the complete opposite, it's liberating. It means freedom and a huge opportunity to get to know yourself. A lot of people can't be on their own and settle for rubbish relationships just to be with someone. Honestly, it's far better to be single and happy than to wake up to someone that you want to slap! Even if you are happily cohabiting, it's important to be you. To live your dreams and if that means doing those things on your own then go for it. There is no point waiting around for someone else.

I would love for you to have a bucket list; it doesn't have to be travel related like mine. It can be anything. You are full of dreams, wants and needs. Never, ever, be afraid to write them down and go about making them a reality. You might have commitments now, but I bet there are things on your list that you could do sooner rather than later if you wanted badly enough.

While you might convince yourself that "I could never do that" of course you can. I am not anything special. I don't possess any secret ingredients that you are missing. I'm just me, the girl with the mousy brown hair who is a bit vertically challenged! The only notable thing I did is, I got honest with myself in more ways than one. I stopped faking life. I quit pretending to be someone I was not. I said "to hell" with the pigeonhole I was trying to squeeze into and started living the way I was meant to.

You don't need to change. You just need to value yourself and know that you are on this earth to make a difference. Stop comparing yourself to others and thinking that I "should be..." There is no "normal," thankfully we live in an age where anything goes.

Besides, people will come and go from your life. Marriages fail, relationships breakup, deaths occur, kids leave the nest, and people naturally drift apart as they follow their own chosen life path. The only person that is with you for your entire journey on this earth is you. So liking yourself, being your own best friend and living every day in harmony with your inner critic is essential. There is no getting away from yourself: I know, I tried.

What shortcuts can I give you to save you pain, tears and torment? I wish that someone had told me:

1.In order to be happy and have fulfilment learn to love yourself. As corny as that might sound, please believe me that it is essential to your total wellbeing and everyone else's that comes into contact with you. Driving yourself mad in your head is a waste of time. There are plenty of people on the planet that will do that for you so why add to it?

2.You are perfectly imperfect, whole and enough. Learn to embrace your uniqueness and strengths and love your quirks. Be yourself and be proud of who you are, there is no one like you on this planet. You do not need anyone's approval, only your own. Your life is what you make of it.

Oscar Wilde famously said, "be yourself, everyone else is taken".

3. You matter too. We can show others kindness and compassion yet we as a society have been told that it is selfish to practise self-care. It's not. Far from it. You wouldn't expect your loved ones not to care about themselves so why would it be any different for you? Take time out if you need to. Speak up for yourself and set boundaries. You may lose friends when you start to show self-worth but that's ok. You need people in your life who value you and want you to be happy.

4.Have fun and lots of it, alone or with others. Find your passion, tribe, hobbies and interests. That's where like minded people will be. Be aware of who drains your energy and who picks you up. Have all the wonderful experiences you can. Make a bucket list and set about ticking boxes off it. You only live once so go for it!

5. Stop comparing yourself to others. Especially the social media version of that person. It's fake and has filters. Nobody is that happy and looks that good all the time. We never see the reality behind their perfect smiles. Your eyes are the windows to your soul, make sure that your eyes are sparkling with life.

If you need inspiration, find those who are posting "real" pictures of themselves and their life. Read biographies of those who you admire. Find others who have overcome adversity. Talk to people who have done what you have always dreamt of doing. Listen to motivational people who stir up your passion.

6. Move towards growth. Like everything on the planet we are here to grow and evolve. There is an old proverb about how stagnant waters breed malaria! Get honest with yourself. Have you ever examined what is working for you and what is not? It takes a lot of courage to sit down and have a progress report with yourself. When we

resist growth and change by being rigid in our thoughts, we deny ourselves an opportunity to learn about ourselves. Being resilient means being able to adapt to whatever life brings your way. Allow your caterpillar to become a butterfly!

7. Heal your past. While that might be easy to say it's not always just as simple as forgiving and forgetting. Some people have had exceptionally traumatic lives or have had horrendous events occur in their lives. While no one is asking you to push what happened under the carpet you may need professional help to find a way forward while living with the pain of the past. Carrying such a burden is only going to inhibit your life and personal development. Healing old wounds is hard but the chance to live a life with dignity and hope is what you deserve. Not more pain. You have been through enough.

8. You are responsible for your own happiness and health. Look after them. No one is here on this earth to be an entertainment system for you. (Likewise you are not responsible for other people's happiness.) Stand on your own two feet and take personal responsibility for your fulfilment and goals.

That includes exercise, fresh air, sleep and what you eat. You are not a machine; there are no spare parts. You have to get your body to the finish line. Think of it as if it were on loan. When you hand it back, do you want to be ashamed of what you did to it!?

9. Ensure you fill your "toolbox" with tools that you can draw on when your inner critic is running riot or times are tough. Everyone is different and you will need to find what works best for you. I adore Life Coaching as it is extremely helpful, it helps you to weed out the nitty gritty in your life and find coping methods that are exclusive to you. I love to journal, draw, talk out loud and record it. Then I can read or listen back and see what "surfaced" for me. Find your own methods, it can be anything so long as it gets you to open up to your feelings, face your inner critic, issues and move onwards.

10. Travel solo, even if just for one day in your own city. Go out and

explore a place with fresh eyes, hang out in tourist traps and see who you get talking to. Never ever wait until you have someone to join you, you have yourself. There is a big world out there filled with interesting, funny and amazing people. Open yourself up to talking to a stranger, you never know what you will learn or what story they have. You might even make a lifelong friend you can visit in some fabulous part of the world.

Solo travelling was by far the best thing I ever did for myself. Stepping outside my life and seeing the world broadened my horizons and showed me what really matters. I found out what I was made of. I had to look out for myself, be my own companion and in turn be my own best friend. In my best hippy dippy catchphrase, I "found myself" thanks to those trips and adventures. Even better, I liked who I discovered. When I stripped back all the bullshit and expectations that I had put on myself, I found a girl with a huge heart who had been buried under a pile of shite!

What I have noticed too, is that when you're happy and at peace with yourself life is much easier too. Things can appear to just fall into place and everyone around you is infected by your vibrancy. Toxic friendships melt away. Energy leeches no longer have a blood supply and empty soulless relationships will crumble. Don't worry, that's a great result!

They will be replaced by people who are on your level and who care about you, the real you. We cannot stand still; any heart specialist will tell you that! You have to keep moving forward. After all, if nothing changed, the world would be full of caterpillars and there would be no butterflies. What a tragedy that would be.

I promise you if you can make quality time for yourself you will hear "your innermost thoughts and feelings." You just have to be willing to listen and take action.

Whatever you do, my wish for you is that you dig deep into your soul. Find love for yourself, be kind to yourself and enjoy your life. It's not a dress rehearsal after all. When you find your smile, wear it with pride. I can't guarantee there will never be ups and downs, it would be naive to think that. But I can promise you that when you have self-worth, self-esteem and a passion for your life, you will be living your best life too.

"We delight in the beauty of the butterfly, but rarely admit the changes it has gone through to achieve that beauty."

-Maya Angelou